GODFATHERS OF CHICAGO'S CHINATOWN

TRIADS, TONGS & STREET GANGS

HARRISON FILLMORE

Published by The History Press
Charleston, SC
www.historypress.com

Original cover artwork by author Harrison Fillmore.

First published 2023

Manufactured in the United States

ISBN 9781467153942

Library of Congress Control Number: 2022950058

A police officer and an unidentified Chinese man in Chinatown community area. Chicago Daily News *collection, Chicago History Museum.*

CONTENTS

Introduction 7

1. The Hit 9
2. Ancient History 13
3. Structure and Organization 20
4. Tongs in Chicago 30
5. Rivalry 50
6. Violence Erupts 55
7. Tong War 61
8. Legitimacy 83
9. Hong Ching: The New Ones 90
10. The Hip Sing Robbery 97
11. Beginning of the End 109
12. The Mob Moves In 114
13. Law Enforcement Catches a Break 117
14. The Raids 131
15. Indictments and Trial 137

Epilogue 141
Notes 147
Bibliography 157
About the Author 160

INTRODUCTION

If Satan came out of the depths of his Inferno, away from the shrieks of the lost millions, he would wander from city to city until he reached Chicago.
Then, in this twentieth century of culture, refinement and progress, he would stand outside the gates, smile in triumph and speak this,—the living, shameful, naked truth:
This is the CITY ACCURSED! This is the CITY OF THE LIVING DAMNED! This is the CITY OF MY DESIRE! This is the CITY AFTER MY OWN HEART! VICE, CRIME, CORRUPTION RULE:—MY TRIUMVIRATE!
This is THE MOST WICKED CITY IN THE WORLD!
Satan would tell the truth.

—*Robert O. Harland,* The Vice Bondage of a Great City or The Most Wicked City in the World

Everyone knows the name Al Capone. There have been volumes written on the infamous organized crime figure. Very few know of Moy Dong Chew, aka Hip Lung, aka "Opium Dong," one of Chinatown's original godfathers. Most folks have heard plenty of stories about the Mafia, the St. Valentine's Day massacre and the gang wars during Prohibition. But there is scant record of the On Leong, the Hip Sings or the Tong Wars during that same time period.

Chinatown has always had a dark and mysterious side. There has always been organized crime, led by colorful characters similar to those of the Mafia. Chicago, in particular, was home to vast criminal enterprises, strictly bound by old country rituals, rules and traditions. To become a member of a Chinatown tong, an applicant attended an ancient ceremony, eerily similar to the initiation to become a "made" member of the Mafia. There was a strict hierarchy in this underworld, controlling everything from the gambling rackets to extortion, prostitution, human trafficking and drug smuggling. Organized crime was rampant in Chicago's Chinatown, hidden behind red and gold restaurant curtains, in backroom gambling haunts and basement opium dens. What seemed strange and exotic to the common *gweilo* (foreign devil) was purposely designed to avert the prying eyes of law enforcement. The language barrier served to further thwart investigations and stall efforts to bring alleged perpetrators to justice. There was an extremely violent side that kept the tongs' criminal enterprise interests profitable. Operating Chinatown's mob took strong-arm tactics, threats and, sometimes, murder. It was a very efficient operation, one that spanned many decades and affected many citizens.

The history of crime in Chinatown follows a similar pattern to that of crime among many immigrant populations. Chicago has a rich history of ethnic organized crime: the Italians, the Jews, the Irish and even the first band of French settlers, who were accused of unfair trading and stealing land. Like most mobs, Chinatown's criminals preyed on their own, rarely impacting victims who weren't ethnic Chinese. Ethnic criminal organizations often began as social service ventures, providing aid and support for their local community. Even Al Capone handed out Easter baskets once in a while. But behind the civic face of these benevolent organizations such as the On Leong was a wicked dragon's tail of corruption and lawlessness.

CHAPTER 1
THE HIT

多行不义必自毙

"PERSISTING IN EVIL LEADS TO SELF-DESTRUCTION"

The Ghost Shadows hid on the balcony of the On Leong Merchants Association building, armed, lying in wait. They had been summoned to Chicago from New York City by Gen Ping Moy, a leader in the On Leong Tong and member of the powerful Moy family. They were there to murder rival Hip Sing Tong member William "Fatman" Chin.[1]

The Moy crime family had run Chicago's Chinatown since its inception in the late 1800s. Members of the Moy family had been unofficial "mayors of Chinatown." Through their On Leong Tong, they ran a criminal syndicate within their community that included gambling, prostitution and the distribution of opium.

Their rivals were the Hip Sing Tong, many of whose members were part of the Chin family. Chicago was unique in that there were essentially two Chinatown neighborhoods. The On Leong Tong controlled the larger, more established Chinatown on the edge of the hardworking, blue-collar Bridgeport neighborhood, and the Hip Sing Tong controlled what was often called New or Little Chinatown on the north side of the city, on the northern border of the diverse and transient neighborhood of Uptown.

On the second of August 1980, Hip Sing Tong members trespassed into rival On Leong Tong–controlled Chinatown territory. They were attempting to extort local restaurant owner Henry Fong, who had already been paying his street tax to the On Leong Tong. Fong resisted and refused the Hip Sing Tong's demands. Just after midnight, Fong was closing up his restaurant at 2243 South Wentworth for the evening when several Hip Sing Tong members forced their way into the restaurant. Fong ran to the back of his restaurant while several members chased him to a back bar. Other members stood guard at the door, and Fong was physically attacked. The Hip Sing members disappeared as quickly as they had arrived. Fong went first to Mercy Hospital, where he was treated for bruises on his face and chest. Next, Fong paid a visit to the On Leong for assistance. Fong identified Hip Sing members William Fatman Chin and Wai Yan Lee as two of his attackers.

The Moy family took quick action. Henry Fong wasn't just some innocent merchant; he was, in fact, a ranking officer in the On Leong. He was very close to current unofficial Chinatown mayor Wilson Moy and was one of the managers of the gang's lucrative underground casino, in which he had a personal financial interest. The Moys contacted associates from New York City, Boston and Pittsburgh and planned a meeting in Chicago. On the eighth of August, the ranking members of the tong met in the On Leong Merchants Association building at 2216 South Wentworth. The situation had to be handled delicately, in the interest of avoiding an all-out war with the Hip Sing Tong. The leaders agreed, however, that committing crimes in rival territory called for action. It was agreed that Ghost Shadow members from New York City would be hired to take care of their problem.

Gen Ping Moy contacted Ghost Shadow member Sik Chin from Mott Street in New York City. Moy provided the money for Sik Chin to purchase airline tickets for himself and other Ghost Shadow members, including Lenny Chow, Willie Chin, David Cheng, Peter Lee, David Lee and John Wong. On Leong Tong member Michael Chan rented a maroon Mercury for the Ghost Shadow members to use during their stay in Chicago. The members were also provided places to stay in Chicago's Chinatown, many of which were the homes of Moy family members.

William Fatman Chin, Hung Mui, Johnson Lee and Wai Yan "Allen" Lee were out on the town on the evening of the ninth of August 1980. They spent most of the evening at a north side disco called the Wizard of Oz in the Old Town neighborhood and didn't leave the establishment until close to three o'clock in the morning. They piled into Fatman's blue two-door Chevrolet and headed into Chinatown.

William Fatman Chin double-parked his car in front of the On Leong Merchants Association building at 2216 South Wentworth. Hung Mui and Johnson Lee exited the vehicle to buy cigarettes. Wai Yan Allen Lee remained in the vehicle. As they waited for their friends, Wai Yan Lee observed a man he knew as "Lenny" up on the On Leong building's balcony. Allen knew Lenny to be a member of the Ghost Shadow gang from New York City's Mott Street crew. Hung Mui and Johnson Lee returned to the vehicle, and Allen took his eyes off the balcony. That's when the shots rang out.

Bullets tore into the vehicle from three different weapons off the On Leong balcony. The windshield shattered with one of the first rounds. Rounds ripped through the car roof and into the driver's side door and armrest. Errant rounds struck a parked car and the plate glass windows of a business across the street. Fatman was struck in the neck and chest. The other three passengers dove from the vehicle and fled the shots.

Chicago police officers Hastings and Macjen were on duty and on routine patrol assigned to the Twenty-First District's paddy wagon when they heard the shots. They arrived to find William Fatman Chin bleeding profusely from

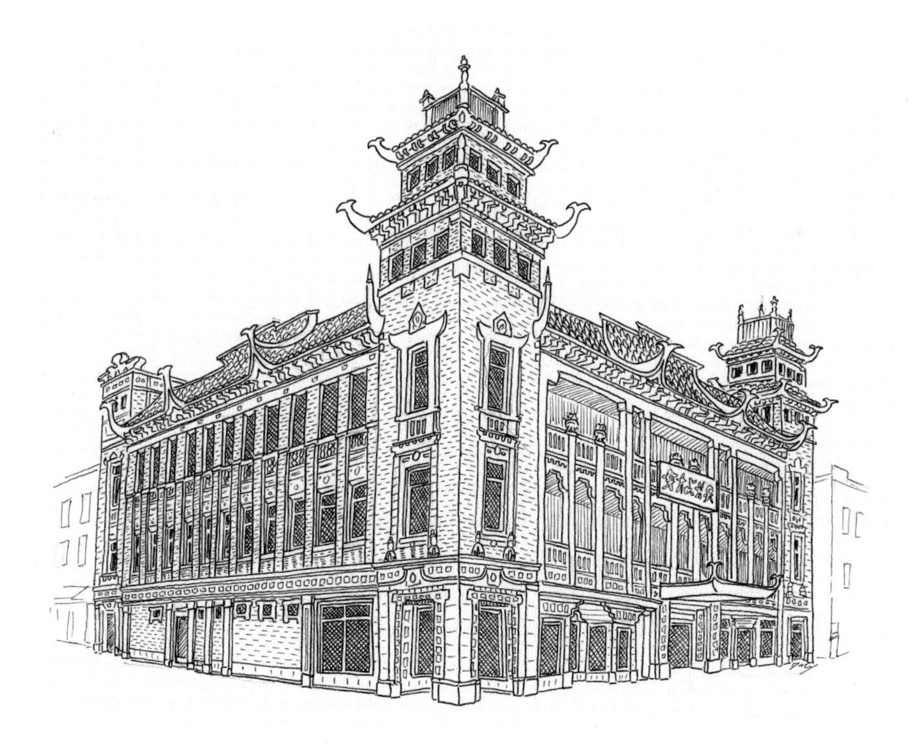

Author's rendering of On Leong Merchants Association building. *Harrison Fillmore.*

gunshot wounds. Fearing that he would not make it in time for an ambulance to respond, they transported him in their squadrol (paddy wagon) to nearby Mercy Hospital.

Chicago Police sex crimes investigators Detectives Finnelly and Perry also happened to be on duty and in the neighborhood when they heard the barrage of gunfire. Responding to the chaotic scene, they learned that the shots had come from the balcony of the On Leong building. With several uniformed officers' assistance, they entered the building as Wai Yan Lee directed them to the balcony from where he believed the shots were fired. On that balcony, investigators found several spent shell casings. In the room adjacent to the balcony, they found Sik Chin.

William Fatman Chin was being prepped for surgery at Mercy Hospital, and detectives had little time to speak with him. He had lost a lot of blood, but in his weakened state, he was able to tell the detectives that members of the Ghost Shadow gang from New York City shot him and was able to identify one of the shooters as "Lenny" before he was rushed into surgery.

William Fatman Chin did not survive.

The murder would lead to the eventual downfall and death knell of the On Leong Tong and organized crime in Chicago's Chinatown.

CHAPTER 2

ANCIENT HISTORY

万事开头难

"All Things Are Difficult at the Start"

It is often difficult to differentiate between fact and legend when it comes to the history of Chinese organized crime. There is a rich history of secret societies formed for rebellion, mutual aid or protection and criminal activity. To understand organized crime in Chicago's Chinatown, it is important to understand the historical significance of these secret societies.

The term "Triad" was coined by British colonialists in Hong Kong to describe the Tiandihui, secret criminal societies. In China, these societies are better known as Hak Sh'e Wui, or Black Societies.[2] "Triad" was derived from the triangular symbolism of heaven, earth and man used by the Heaven and Earth Society, otherwise known as the Tin Tei Wui. During conflicts, the Black Societies would fly black banners displaying the Hung character within a red triangle. Short for *hongmen*, meaning "vast family," the Hung character is also loosely translated as "authentic."

Chinese secret societies began well before British rule and are said to have served as underground movements supporting the former Ming dynasty to overthrow the Machu Qing dynasty in the seventeenth century. According to legend, the Qing emperor Qianlong requested the assistance of 128 Shaolin monks to battle an invading army of Xi Lu barbarians. The monks were successful in fighting off the invading force, preserving Qing dynasty

Top: Author's rendering of the Hongmen triangle. *Harrison Fillmore.*

Bottom: Members of a Chinese secret society after being charged in court. *Country of Thailand, public domain.*

territory. The emperor offered a reward of riches to the monks, but they refused, choosing instead to go back to their monastery and their holy devotions of prayer and poverty. The outraged emperor sent his army to raid and destroy the monastery and execute the monks. Five monks escaped the deadly ambush, vowing revenge and creating the rebel movement.

Stories and legends exist of several colorful secret societies, one of the earliest being the Red Eyebrows, who were known for painting their foreheads red before battle.[3] The movement began as a rebellion against the Xing dynasty after a combination of natural disasters and a sudden increase in taxes by leader Wang Man threatened peasants with starvation. The Red Eyebrows dyed their foreheads before forming raiding parties, pillaging villages loyal to Wang Man and government resources.

A self-appointed mystic named Chang Chueh began a secret society called the Yellow Turbans to oppose the Han dynasty. Chueh led his organization with *t'ai p'ing*, an ancient brand of magic and superstitions. His followers believed that the Yellow Turbans were destined to overthrow the Han dynasty and, in doing so, change the very color of the sky from blue to yellow.[4] Although the organization would eventually self-destruct from infighting and the rise of Buddhism, it was ultimately successful in eliminating the Han dynasty.

The White Lotus Society grew during the Sung dynasty and became one of the leading factors in the overthrow of the Mongol Yuan dynasty. The organization had several offshoots and smaller sects including the White Lilies, the White Yangs and the Incense Smellers.[5] They were connected to the Heaven and Earth Society and performed many of the same rituals. White Lotus leader Han Shand-Tung was the recognized leader until a Buddhist monk named Chu Yuan-Chang took over and became the Hung Wu emperor. In establishing the Ming dynasty, he ultimately outlawed the White Lotus altogether. However, the secret society continued underground and later paved the way to overthrow the Ming dynasty in 1629, throwing their support the way of the Manchu Qing dynasty.

The Society of God Worshippers was led by a man who by most accounts was deemed sickly and insane.[6] Hung Hsiu-ch'üan led the faction, borrowing myths and traditions from Buddhism, Tao and Christianity. This lower-level sect was originally supported by the larger Triads for its usefulness in maintaining secrecy and in the goal of overthrowing the Qing dynasty in favor of the Ming. The group would be a major influence in beginning the Taiping Rebellion. After the rebellion, the Triads had little use for the zealous sect. Under suspicious circumstances, Hung Hsiu-ch'üan committed suicide.

Above: Author's faithful reproduction of a Qing dynasty illustration of Liu Bei, Guan Yu and Zhang Fei during the 184 CE Yellow Turban Rebellion in China. *Scholars of Chenzhou.*

Left: Depiction of the White Lotus Society, artist unknown, 1041–1106. *Courtesy of the Met Museum.*

Author's rendering of Du Tuesheng, aka "Big Eared Du." *Harrison Fillmore.*

Another smaller faction under the larger Triad organization called itself the Small Swords. Also involved in the Taiping Rebellion, this particularly violent sect led the revolt in Shanghai. It was responsible for robberies and kidnappings to intimidate the Chinese residents into cooperating with its rebellion. Civilians who did not cooperate or were suspected of aiding the enemy were beaten and tortured. Shanghai residents who had had enough formed an opposition group of vigilantes, calling themselves the Shanghai Volunteer Corp. The SVC, as it was known, soon outgrew the Small Swords. Due to the brutal tactics of the Small Swords, and possibly sensing opportunity, other factions of Triad organizations, such as the Green Gang and the Red Gang, threw their support behind the SVC. Eventually, the Small Swords were driven out of Shanghai for good. Once they were ousted, the other factions soon took over the organized criminal activity.

The Green Gang was a group of criminals organized by Du Tuesheng, otherwise known as "Big Eared Du." Once the Small Swords were vanquished, Du and his Green Gang began smuggling and selling opium, trafficking large quantities into the United States. Du Tuesheng and his Green Gang became successful through his political and military influences in the Kuomintang party, which ruled from 1912 until after World War II. According to a Chinese organized crime writer, "[Du Tueshung and] Shanghai in the 1930s made the Chicago of Al Capone appear a staid, almost, provincial town."[7]

The Boxer Rebellion was largely supported by the Fists of Righteous Harmony, or the I Ho Chuan. The British simply called the Triad-associated faction Boxers, given their effectiveness in martial arts and hand-to-hand combat.[8] The bloody rebellion was eventually quashed by government forces with the aid of outside armies. Other influential groups included the Big Swords, the Red Spears and the Heavenly Dragons.[9]

The Tiandihui, or Heaven and Earth Society, began in 1761 as a benevolent organization created for mutual aid. There were four original founders of the Tiandihui: Ti Xi, Li Amin, Zhu Dingyuan and Tao Yuan. They were the first to claim that the organization was founded by the Five

Left: Photograph of Boxer Rebels circa 1900. *Togo Shrine and Togo Association.*

Right: Officers of the Six Companies. *From the Roy D. Graves Collection, Chinese and Chinatown, Bancroft Library, University of California, Berkeley.*

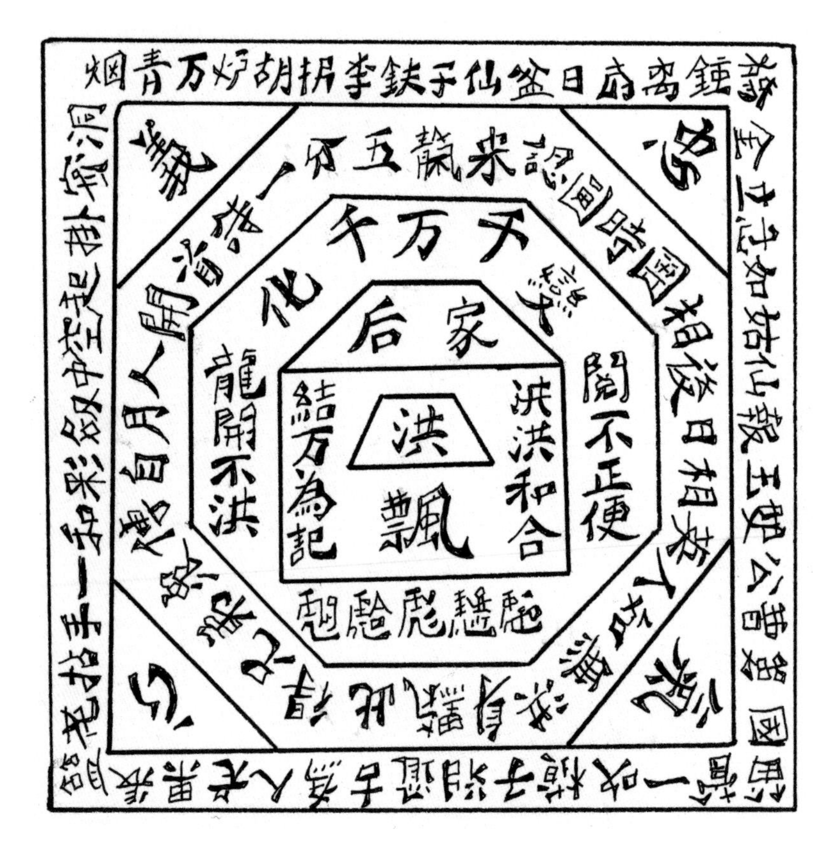

Author's rendering of the Heaven and Earth Society, Hongmen scroll from the nineteenth century. *Harrison Fillmore.*

Shaolin Monks. Also known as Hung Mun, or Hongmen, the secret society became a refuge for revolutionaries. Robberies and kidnappings became its primary sources for funding these conflicts.[10]

The society's name was later changed to Sam Hop Wui, the Three United Society, or Triads, to the British. When groups of Hongmen began to form in the United States, they began to call themselves Chinese Freemasons. Soon, Triads became synonymous with all of Chinese organized crime.

CHAPTER 3

STRUCTURE AND ORGANIZATION

邪门歪道

"Evil Folks and Crooked Ways"

Triads were structured organizations. They were shrouded in mystery and influenced deeply by superstition and old-world traditions. The number 4 became a holy number to the Triads, representing the four oceans that surround the mainland. Each rank of the Triad hierarchy is numerically symbolic, all beginning with the number 4. Number 489 represents the Dragon Head or Shan Chu. The Dragon Head was the leader of the entire Triad. He had final say over any disputes, and while he held what was considered an "elected" position, his decisions were not up for debate. The Dragon Head has also been called Mountain Lord and referred to as the number 21, being the sum of all three number characters in his title added together.

Directly under the power of the Dragon Head was the White Paper Fan, or Pak Tsz Sin, of his choosing. This position was of great importance to the Dragon Head but held no official power within the ranks of the organization. The White Paper Fan was in charge of politics and policy, all under the scepter of the Dragon Head. The position is often compared to the Italian Mafia's position of consigliere.

Under the Dragon Head were three positions of equal power, represented by the number 438. The Assistant Mountain Lord, the Incense Master

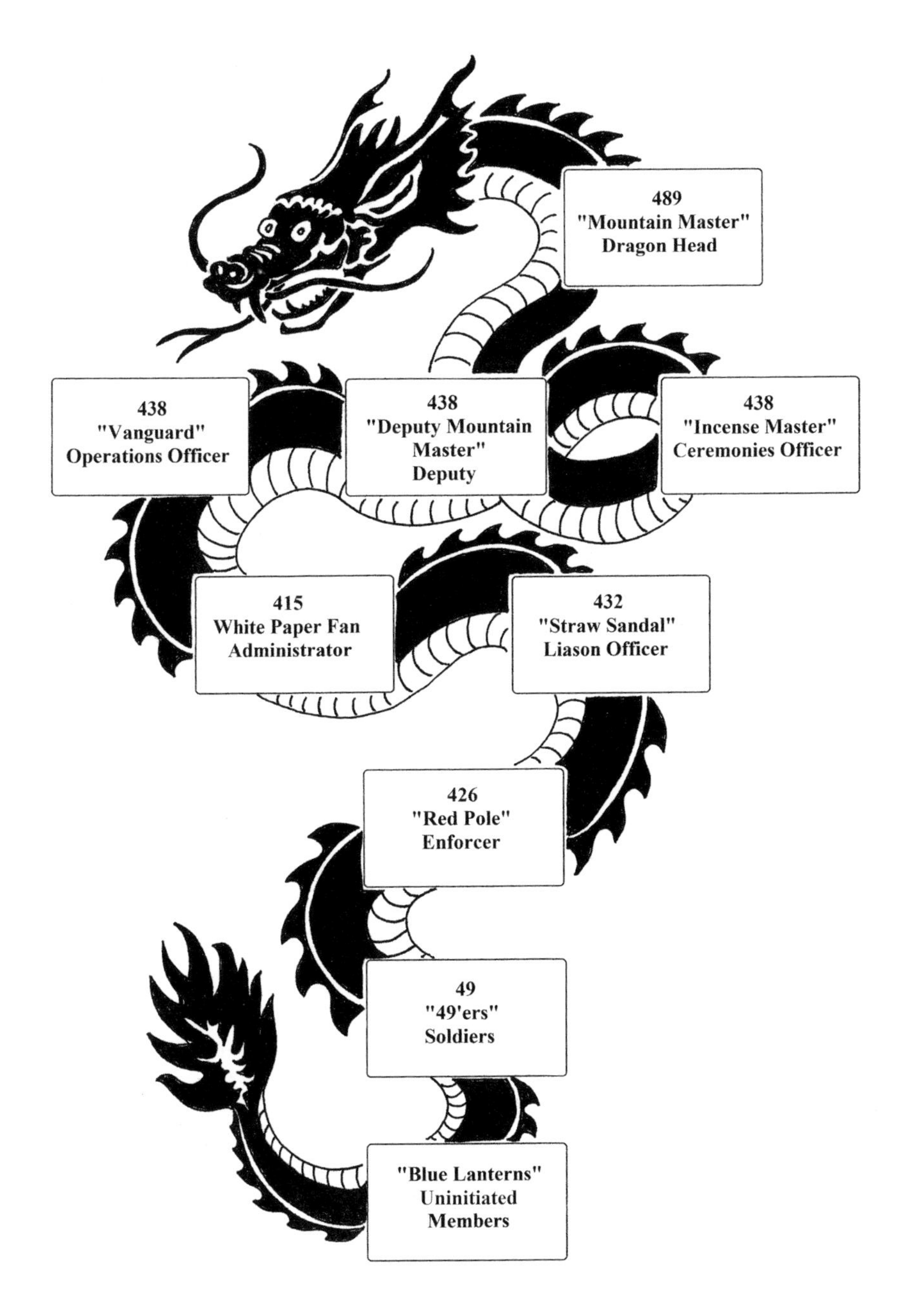

Author's rendering of a traditional Triad hierarchy chart. *Harrison Fillmore.*

and the Vanguard, despite their equal status in the hierarchy, had different responsibilities. The Assistant Mountain Lord, or Fu San Chu, was the Dragon Head's real proxy and acted like the right-hand man of the Dragon Head. He was often consulted about decisions by the Dragon Head and could hand out orders as such.

The Incense Master, or Hueng Chu, and the Vanguard, or Sin Fung, were the masters of all rituals. They were in charge of all the secret society's traditions and ongoing rituals. They supervised induction ceremonies and were in charge of the overall chain of command. They were also the decision makers and the ranking members responsible for deciding and then carrying out punishment as they saw fit.

Beneath these three powerful ranking members were several other ranks with varying duties. The Messenger's, or Cho Hai's, duties included making certain that all members were informed of recent decisions, goals and other information that needed to be disseminated among the members. He was also the debt collector from the different tribes and sects. The Cho Hai would then hand over everything to the Treasurer, or Cha So, who was responsible for the bookkeeping within the organization.

The Red Pole was the enforcer of the organization. He was in charge of keeping the organization's members trained. He kept them in line through harsh discipline. The Red Pole was expected to lead the members in battle and was in charge of the overall, everyday workings of the rank and file.

Triads were composed of several smaller factions. Those sects were led by a Chu Chui. Each Chu Chui had a second-in-command called the Fu Chu Chui. These smaller factions each had their own names, traditions and rituals but were ultimately loyal to and ruled by the larger Triads. At the bottom of the hierarchy were the foot soldiers called Sze Kau.

To become a member of a Triad, if one was not forced into the ranks, prospective foot soldiers first had to find a sponsor. A new member was required to have a full-fledged, and sometimes ranking, member vouch for their entry into the secret society. The full-fledged member was called the Dai Lo, or Big Brother. The prospect was therefore the Sai Lo, or Little Brother. Because of the nature of the brotherly organization, the Big and Little Brothers were always connected in some way. The Big Brother was responsible for his Little Brother's loyalty and ensured that his needs were met. It could be years before the Little Brother became a Big Brother, with a Sai Lo of his own.

Normally, a hefty entrance fee was required. The Incense Master and Vanguard were responsible for a background check on each prospective

Author's faithful reproduction of a front-page illustration from the *Call* newspaper (San Francisco), January 2, 1898: "Initiation." *Original artist unknown.*

member. The rigorous process of testing the loyalty and affiliations of the applicant could take weeks. If finally accepted, the prospective member attended a three-day holy ceremony.

For three days, a prospect was subjected to tests of loyalty and threatened with violence if he should break that loyalty. As final preparations were arranged, the member was prepared for what was normally a six-hour induction ceremony, which would include other prospective members. If the prospective member was granted final approval, he received an invitation to the ritual written on bamboo in red ink.

Prospective members were made to strip, including shoes and socks, then adorned in traditional Buddhist garb with chest bared. They were led through a symbolic gate on which was inscribed, "Upon entering the door, do not proceed further if you are not loyal."[11] A ritual dance was performed as the prospect walked into a four-walled ritual room, smoke-filled with incense and

Author's rendering of a bamboo invitation to join a secret society. *Harrison Fillmore.*

ringing with the banging of gongs. Within the room stood three more symbolic gates through which the prospect must pass. The first was a gate of crossed swords, called the Passing of the Mountain of Knives.[12] After the prospects passed through, the Vanguard would formally add their names to the membership books.

The second gate was called the Loyalty and Righteousness Hall, with the inscription, "Before the gate of loyalty and righteousness all men are equal." Once through this gate, the prospect paid his final initiation fee and was given a small red envelope in return. The final gate was the Heaven and Earth Circle. The gate was a bamboo hoop the prospect passed through, symbolizing his rebirth as a member of the Triad. Inscribed on that gate were the words, "Through Heaven and Earth Circle are born the Hung Heroes." From here the initiates began the ritual and were subjected to a series of acts that symbolized the Triad's traditions and history. Under the careful eye of senior Triad members, the initiates were led through obstacles such as the Stepping Stones, the Two Plank Bridge and, finally, the Fiery Pit. If they were successful, the final ritual began.[13]

Successful initiates were made to stand at an altar. They were formally introduced to the hierarchy of the Triad. Ranking members of the Triad would "bless" the initiates by reciting secret poetry for every member. The initiates were once again stripped, made to wash and given white robes and straw sandals. Blood was drawn from the arms of each member and dripped into a holy urn. Once every member's blood was collected, the initiates would recite the thirty-six oaths to Kwan Yu, the god of secret oaths. The thirty-six oaths are as follows:

> *After having entered the Hung gates I must treat the parents and relatives of my sworn brothers as my own kin. I shall suffer death by five thunderbolts if I do not keep this oath.*

I shall assist my sworn brothers to bury their parents and brothers by offering financial or physical assistance. I shall be killed by five thunderbolts if I pretend to have no knowledge of their troubles.

When Hung brothers visit my house, I shall provide them with board and lodging. I shall be killed by myriads of knives if I treat them as strangers.

I will always acknowledge my Hung brothers when they identify themselves. If I ignore them I will be killed by myriads of swords.

I shall not disclose the secrets of the Hung family, not even to my parents, brothers, or wife. I shall never disclose the secrets for money. I will be killed by myriads of swords if I do so.

I shall never betray my sworn brothers. If, through a misunderstanding, I have caused the arrest of one of my brothers I must release him immediately. If I break this oath I will be killed by five thunderbolts.

I will offer financial assistance to sworn brothers who are in trouble in order that they may pay their passage fee, etc. If I break this oath I will be killed by five thunderbolts.

I must never cause harm or bring trouble to my sworn brothers or Incense Master. If I do so I will be killed by myriads of swords.

I must never commit any indecent assaults on the wives, sisters, or daughters of my sworn brothers. I shall be killed by five thunderbolts if I break this oath.

I shall never embezzle cash or property from my sworn brothers. If I break this oath I will be killed by myriads of swords.

I will take good care of the wives or children of sworn brothers entrusted to my keeping. If I do not I will be killed by five thunderbolts.

If I have supplied false particulars about myself for the purpose of joining the Hung family I shall be killed by five thunderbolts.

If I should change my mind and deny my membership of the Hung family I will be killed by myriads of swords.

If I rob a sworn brother or assist an outsider to do so I will be killed by five thunderbolts.

If I should take advantage of a sworn brother or force unfair business deals upon him I will be killed by myriads of swords.

If I knowingly convert my sworn brother's cash or property to my own use I shall be killed by five thunderbolts.

If I have wrongly taken a sworn brother's cash or property during a robbery I must return them to him. If I do not I will be killed by five thunderbolts.

If I am arrested after committing an offence I must accept my punishment and not try to place blame on my sworn brothers. If I do so I will be killed by five thunderbolts.

If any of my sworn brothers are killed, or arrested, or have departed to some other place, I will assist their wives and children who may be in need. If I pretend to have no knowledge of their difficulties I will be killed by five thunderbolts.

When any of my sworn brothers have been assaulted or blamed by others, I must come forward and help him if he is in the right or advise him to desist if he is wrong. If he has been repeatedly insulted by others I shall inform our other brothers and arrange to help him physically or financially. If I do not keep this oath I will be killed by five thunderbolts.

If it comes to my knowledge that the Government is seeking any of my sworn brothers who has come from other provinces or from overseas, I shall immediately inform him in order that he may make his escape. If I break this oath I will be killed by five thunderbolts.

I must not conspire with outsiders to cheat my sworn brothers at gambling. If I do so I will be killed by myriads of swords.

I shall not cause discord amongst my sworn brothers by spreading false reports about any of them. If I do so I will be killed by myriads of swords.

I shall not appoint myself as Incense Master without authority. After entering the Hung gates for three years the loyal and faithful ones may be promoted by the Incense Master with the support of his sworn brothers. I shall be killed by five thunderbolts if I make any unauthorized promotions myself.

If my natural brothers are involved in a dispute or lawsuit with my sworn brothers I must not help either party against the other but must attempt to have the matter settled amicably. If I break this oath I will be killed by five thunderbolts.

After entering the Hung gates I must forget any previous grudges I may have borne against my sworn brothers. If I do not do so I will be killed by five thunderbolts.

I must not trespass upon the territory occupied by my sworn brothers. I shall be killed by five thunderbolts if I pretend to have no knowledge of my brothers' rights in such matters.

I must not covet or seek to share any property or cash obtained by my sworn brothers. If I have such ideas I will be killed.

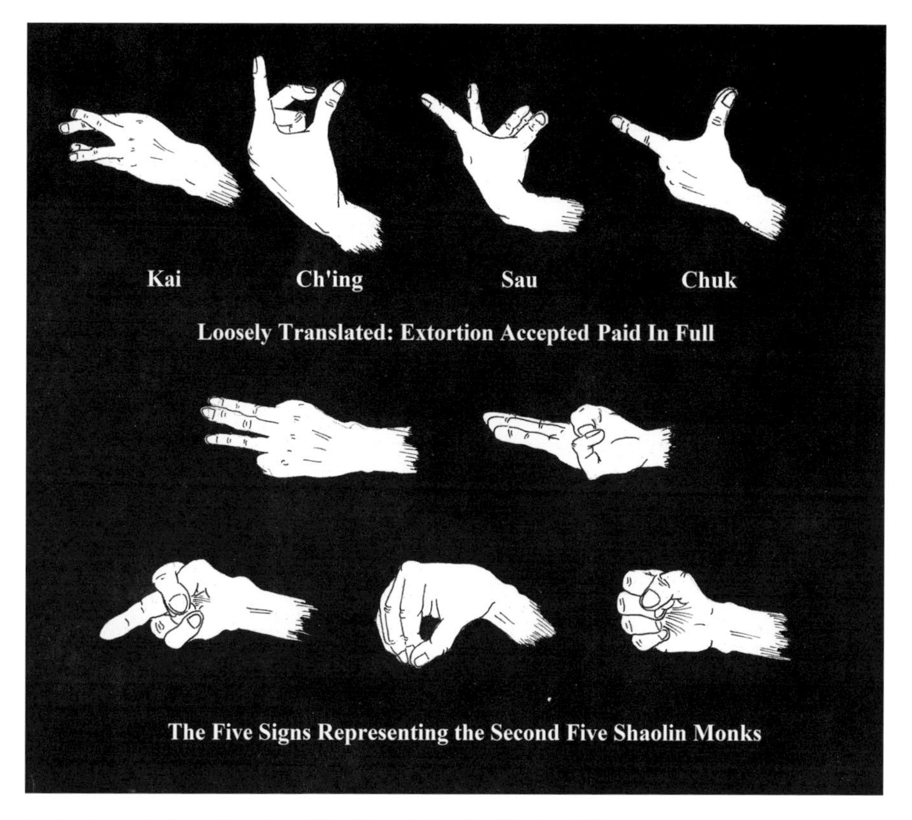

Author's rendering of ancient Triad hand signals. *Harrison Fillmore.*

I must not disclose any address where my sworn brothers keep their wealth nor must I conspire to make wrong use of such knowledge. If I do so I will be killed by myriads of swords.

I must not give support to outsiders if doing so is against the interests of any of my sworn brothers. If I do not keep this oath I will be killed by myriads of swords.

I must not take advantage of the Hung brotherhood in order to oppress or take violent or unreasonable advantage of others. I must be content and honest. If I break this oath I will be killed by five thunderbolts.

I shall be killed by five thunderbolts if I behave indecently towards small children of my sworn brothers' families.

If any of my sworn brothers has committed a big offence I must not inform upon them to the Government for the purposes of obtaining a reward. I shall be killed by five thunderbolts if I break this oath.

In 1991, the Permanent Subcommittee on Investigations held a hearing before the Committee on Government Affairs in the United States Senate. The hearing was intended to address the growing problem of Asian organized crime. During that hearing, the testimony of Kenneth Chu, aka "Johnny Wong," was admitted into the record. Having cooperated in a long-term investigation, Chu was offered protection under the federal government's Witness Protection Program and was living under a new identity. Chu described the process of becoming a member of the Ghost Shadow gang in great detail, including details of how the ceremony mirrored the ancient practices.

Chu told the committee that he originally resisted the recruitment to become a street gang member, but after suffering beatings and extortion for having no affiliation to any gang, he submitted and joined.

Two weeks after joining the street gang, Chu was initiated into the On Leong Tong, along with a dozen other members of the Ghost Shadow gang. Chu described the initiation as a ceremony involving burning incense and taking oaths of loyalty, protection and a code of silence. Chu stated that all the Ghost Shadow gang members were also members of the On Leong Tong; however, the On Leong also had legitimate members, business owners and people of Chinese descent with no affiliation to organized crime.

Chu began as a foot soldier in the organization. He was tasked with protecting gambling houses. He and his fellow Ghost Shadow members were not allowed to carry weapons, but they were always nearby. He was paid thirty-five dollars a week through the On Leong Tong, but the real advantage was never having to pay for a meal again, as long as the restaurant was within On Leong territory. The Ghost Shadows also supplemented their income by extorting and occasionally robbing other citizens and business owners.

The On Leong Tong had an extensive national network. Chu stated that after he shot a rival gang member, the organization gave him "long pay" at ninety dollars a week, a reward for having done his duty as a gang member. Chu was also moved to a different city where On Leong connections gave him new credentials and a new identity, hiding him from the local police and prosecution.

Chu was given employment by the On Leong and became a dealer in an underground casino. After a cheating scandal, he and other gang members were ostracized, causing an internal rivalry. Chu eventually ended up in Houston in charge of several gambling rings. When he learned the On Leong Tong had put a hit out on him, open to any member that murdered Chu, he decided to begin working with law enforcement and eventually turned state's evidence.*

* U.S. Congress, *Asian Organized Crime: Hearing before the Senate Permanent Subcommittee on Investigations of the Committee on Governmental Affairs, 102nd Congress, 1st Session, October 3, November 5–6, 1991* (Washington, D.C.: U.S. Government Printing Office, 1992), 30.

I must not take to myself the wives and concubines of my sworn brothers nor commit adultery with them. If I do so I will be killed by myriads of swords.

I must never reveal Hung secrets or signs when speaking to outsiders. If I do so I will be killed by myriads of swords.

After entering the Hung gates I shall be loyal and faithful and shall endeavour to overthrow Ch'ing and restore Ming by coordinating my efforts with those of my sworn brethren even though my brethren and I may not be in the same professions. Our common aim is to avenge our Five Ancestors.[14]

Once the oath was completed, yellow paper was burned and the ashes were mixed into the members' blood. As a ritual of sacrifice, a rooster was killed, and its blood was also mixed into the holy urn. Finally, wine was mixed into the concoction, and every initiate then drank from the urn, symbolizing the sharing of blood among the secret brotherhood.[15]

The initiates had now become Forty-Nines, the lowest rank within the Triads. They were taught secret hand symbols. They learned how to recognize other members by the way they ate their food with chopsticks and how they held and paid money to others. They were formally introduced to all in attendance, and a celebration was held.

CHAPTER 4

TONGS IN CHICAGO

先到先得

"The First to Arrive Is the First to Succeed"

The very first Chinese immigrants arrived in Chicago in 1870.[16] Wah Lee, who for all intents and purposes was the leader of the small group of five immigrants, opened a laundry at 455 South Wabash. One man did the washing, another the ironing, one man kept the books and the two others did the deliveries and collections.[17] The business quickly flourished as it gained a reputation for promptness and efficiency. The Chinese population in Chicago grew in that same decade.

Wah Lee became a colorful character in Chicago's growing Chinatown. His first arrest was for "swindling," according to newspaper accounts.[18] He and four other laundrymen were caught overcharging some customers and billing others for work they'd never ordered. The men were all arrested in the basement of an establishment called the Adams House on the corner of Clark and Harrison and brought to the Armory for arraignment. Purportedly, one of Wah Lee's victims was a member of the Chicago Police Department, perhaps predicting the tumultuous relationship he would have with the police for years to come. Judge Boyden found all parties guilty, and each man was fined ten dollars.

The laundryman soon became a victim himself as he was conducting business with a woman named Mrs. Field, aka Rebecca Green. As the two argued about the price of Mrs. Field's weekly wash, she snatched six dollars from Wah Lee's hand and attempted to abscond with both the stolen cash and her cleaned laundry. Wah Lee, who was skeptical of police involvement, put his skepticism aside, followed Mrs. Field out of his laundry and into the streets and yelled for a policeman. A nearby policeman on foot patrol heard Wah Lee's calls for help and promptly arrested the woman. While she was being processed in the Armory, it was discovered that Mrs. Field, aka Rebecca Green, was wanted on an outstanding arrest warrant.[19]

In 1884, during one of the very first Chinese New Year celebrations in Chicago, Wah Lee was chosen as the spokesman for his people and was interviewed by a reporter. He explained that the Chinese New Year is a merry celebration. The gods Gwan and Kung, of fortune and war, are honored with artwork and the color red. They enjoy a banquet of chicken and rice and other delicacies and, he admitted—with some prodding from the reporter—beer and whiskey, too.[20]

Wah Lee became known not only to the local businessmen but also to police and politicians as the recognized leader of the Celestials. The romanticized name came from early reporters, as the poetic name for China was Tianchao, meaning Celestial Empire. Wah Lee was a fixer and arguably the very first unofficial mayor of Chicago's Chinatown.

Ab Hen of 245 West Madison Street was a madman, or so believed anyone who knew him in and around Chinatown. He was forty years old and had been in Chicago for only five years but had already gained a reputation for being a menace to the good name of Chicago's Chinatown. Wah Lee, assuming his leadership role, arranged to send the man back to China. With a large crowd accompanying him and with newspaper reporters in tow to prove his good intentions, Wah Lee brought the man to Union Station to catch a train to San Francisco. From there, Wah Lee was to place Ab Hen on the first ship back to China, in an effort to improve the madman's morals.[21]

Besides his flourishing laundry business, Wah Lee was running a gambling house at 313 South State Street. According to police reports, Chicago police officers assigned to the Harrison Street Station raided the den and attempted to arrest the men for playing a dice game called "chafe" for money. The raid became chaotic as one man threw a lantern, injuring one of the officers. Four other men jumped out of windows. One man was found hiding in a closet, and still another concealed himself in a steamer trunk. Fifteen Chinese men were arrested in total, and Wah Lee was charged as the keeper of the house.[22]

Chinese labor headquarters. Chicago Daily News *Collection, Chicago History Museum.*

Wah Lee's next run-in with Chicago cops put him on the defensive. According to newspaper reports, Wah Lee was accosted by "tobacco-spurting, Chinese-baiting police officers."[23] As he walked past the Cottage Grove police station, two men taunted him, called him a "rat eater" and told him to go back to China.[24] When Wah Lee began to defend himself, one of the men spat tobacco on his fine coat. Wah Lee then began to yell for the aid of a policeman. That's when the two men identified themselves as cops and promptly arrested Wah Lee.

Early Immigrant Portrait of Li Moy, Gio F. 333 West Madison Avenue Chicago. *Library of Congress, National Archives.*

Wah Lee was quickly bailed out by friends, and after the story came out, a flurry of support came from the press, the public and, of all places, the law. Judge Bradwell presided over the hearing the following Monday. Wah Lee was flanked by the support of the superintendent of the Chinese Christian Sunday School, Cook County commissioner Addison Ballard, Cook County judge Clifford and the head of the First Presbyterian Church.

The officers denied Wah Lee's version of events and told the judge they only arrested him after he threatened to have they themselves arrested. Judge Bradwell found Wah Lee not guilty and made a public statement that he would be forwarding the officers' names for disciplinary purposes to Chicago police chief Brennen.[25]

Wah Lee's last run-in with Chicago police came after he was robbed at gunpoint by a juvenile gang of street toughs. Wah Lee quickly turned the tables on his would-be robbers and, with several other Chinese men, chased them out of his laundry. Two officers alerted by the commotion responded to the scene, but amid the chaos, and because of his overzealous actions, Wah Lee himself was arrested and charged with disorderly conduct. The case was publicized and quickly dismissed, with the department all but apologizing for the mix-up.[26]

It's important to note the location of the first Chinese immigrants. They settled in a neighborhood known as Little Cheyenne due to its Wild West lawlessness and residents' propensity to settle things with a gun. The district was part of the infamously corrupt First Ward under the notorious leadership of John "Hinky Dink" McKenna and "Bathhouse" John Coughlin. The Kenna Saloon served as their headquarters and was directly below one of the city's first Chinese restaurants, the King Yen Lo. The neighborhood was also known as a "tenderloin district" and the "gateway" to the Levee, a wide-open red-light district in Chicago.

As the Chinese population grew, so, too, did their customs, habits and vices. Opium began to seep into the city. Opium dens were hidden all over Chicago's Chinatown, above legitimate laundries and in the basements of saloons. The busiest opium den operated in a decrepit building on the corner of Harrison and Clark Streets. The den was described as having a foul stench from the fetid air; the dirty, cracked, bare walls; and the uncarpeted, unswept

Photograph of an opium den. *Library of Congress, National Archives.*

floors. The rooms were dimly lit with smoky kerosene lamps. Pale addicts with sunken cheeks shivered while lazily inhaling opium from bamboo pipes. Notably, while the majority of customers were Chinese, others came from ethnicities found all over the city and from nearly every walk of life.[27]

The Chicago Police Department credits the very first influx of opium to a man known only as "Crooked Back Jim," a member of the Six Companies Tong. According to law enforcement, Crooked Back Jim came into Chicago in the 1870s for the purpose of introducing the population to opium smoking and to promote the use and sale thereof.[28]

Reformer Reverend John Rusk carried what he claimed to be the original opium pipe, said to have belonged to Crooked Back Jim, which he used as a prop in his sermons while denouncing godlessness, wicked virtues and vice. He himself was too radical for his own church, the Fullerton Avenue Presbyterian Church, and members decided to ostracize him from the congregation. Reverend Rusk, along with close to two thousand converts, left the Presbyterians to form his own Christ Militant Church.[29]

Crooked Back Jim may have very well been nothing but a legend, an imaginary scapegoat for the growing opium trade.

Jim Lee and Charley Ling were federally charged with opium trafficking in 1914. What made the arrests shocking was the evidence the government presented that the dope runners were using Western Union Telegraph messenger boys as mules. Operating out of their "hop joint" at 2821 South Dearborn, the two opium dealers transported their narcotics all over Chinatown and the rest of the red-light district using the youths as cover through all hours of the night.[30]

Government agents for the Department of Revenue attempted to keep the growing opium problem under control. In the fall of 1914, they conducted multiple raids of opium dens in the heart of Chinatown. Six men were arrested, but it was the statement of one arrestee, Lee Hing, that brought more attention to the scale of the operation. Hing related to authorities that, while disguised as a laundryman, he would deliver the dope to his "aristocratic hop customers" in all parts of the city.[31]

Agent Jack Denison of the Internal Revenue Department's narcotics squad was shot during a raid of a local opium den. According to newspaper reports, the agent arrested a smuggler from Kansas City who was trafficking opium into Chicago's Chinatown. When the agent went to the address expecting the delivery, he was met with a "fusillade of bullets."[32] The agent grabbed his arrestee, using the man as a human shield as he advanced. Seven more men were arrested on the premises. Agent Denison survived the attack, but the incident brought to light the dangers of the opium trade and the lengths to which the traffickers would go in order to protect their racket.

A Chinese woman named Fan Toy was the first Chinese madam in Chicago. She ran the brothel above Chow Tai's restaurant, which itself had been raided several times by police for gambling and opium and for harboring a child. Chow Tai and his ex-convict partner Wong Sam had organized a tong known as Kow Lung.[33] That tong lasted a short time before being absorbed by the mightier On Leong.

Chow Tai was also the unofficial undertaker in Chinatown. It was common for a Chinese immigrant's dying wish to be that they were laid to rest back in their home country. Chow Tai provided such a service. He collected the bodies over time until he had enough to turn a profit, charging anywhere between $1,000 and $3,000. Chow Tai hired a special transport to bring each load of filled coffins to San Francisco, where they were then stacked onto a steamship bound for China. For those who couldn't afford the posthumous trip back to China, Chow Tai purchased plots en masse in the far north side cemetery of Rosehill. He also purchased a large obelisk to be erected to honor the dead. The land and monument were funded by the On Leong Tong.

Alice Tong, doubtless not her real name, was another madam in Chinatown. She ran a brothel at 532 South Federal Street. She was arrested in 1914 and

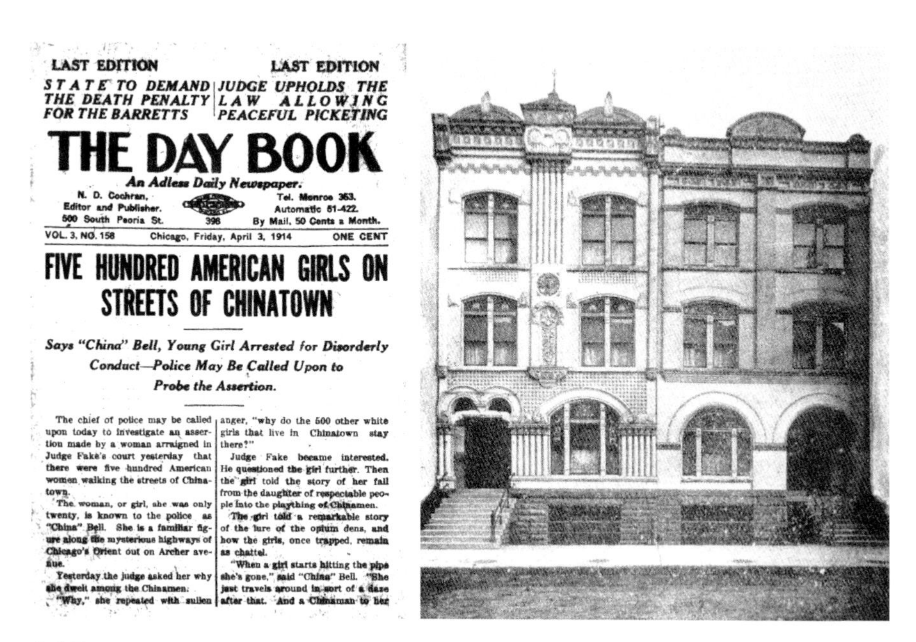

LAST EDITION LAST EDITION

STATE TO DEMAND THE DEATH PENALTY FOR THE BARRETTS

JUDGE UPHOLDS THE LAW ALLOWING PEACEFUL PICKETING

THE DAY BOOK

An Adless Daily Newspaper.

N. D. Cochran, Editor and Publisher. 500 South Peoria St. 398 Tel. Monroe 363. Automatic 51-422. By Mail, 50 Cents a Month.

VOL. 3, NO. 158 Chicago, Friday, April 3, 1914 ONE CENT

FIVE HUNDRED AMERICAN GIRLS ON STREETS OF CHINATOWN

Says "China" Bell, Young Girl Arrested for Disorderly Conduct—Police May Be Called Upon to Probe the Assertion.

The chief of police may be called upon today to investigate an assertion made by a woman arraigned in Judge Fake's court yesterday that there were five hundred American women walking the streets of Chinatown.

The woman, or girl, she was only twenty, is known to the police as "China" Bell. She is a familiar figure along the mysterious highways of Chicago's Orient out on Archer avenue.

Yesterday the judge asked her why she dwelt among the Chinamen.

"Why," she repeated with sullen anger, "why do the 500 other white girls that live in Chinatown stay there?"

Judge Fake became interested. He questioned the girl further. Then the girl told the story of her fall from the daughter of respectable people into the plaything of Chinamen.

The girl told a remarkable story of the lure of the opium dens, and how the girls, once trapped, remain as chattel.

"When a girl starts hitting the pipe she's gone," said "China" Bell. "She just travels around in sort of a daze after that. And a Chinaman to her

Left: Front-page headlines. Day Book *(Chicago), April 3, 1914.*

Right: The Everleigh club. *Originally published by Minna Everleigh, 1911.*

charged with disorderly conduct, along with a man named George Tow.[34] A year later, the Chicago Police Department raided her establishment for being a "house of ill repute."[35]

Another early proprietor of Chinese brothels and an admitted human trafficker was Ng Ying Song. Song would later become the leader of one of the major tongs in the nation, but before he rose to that power, he smuggled "girls" from China to work as prostitutes in his Chicago Chinatown brothels.[36]

Human trafficking became a problem in the city of Chicago, and Chinatown brothels were not excluded. Chicago police arrested a man named Wah Lee Mon for human trafficking after he was caught traveling to Chicago with a fifteen-year-old girl. The girl, named Lizzie Scott, was originally a runaway from Providence, Rhode Island, when she met up with Mon. The couple raised suspicions during their travels back to Chicago since mixed-race couples were rare at the time and because of the couple's age difference. Once confronted by authorities, the victim admitted to being sexually assaulted by Mon, who was charged and taken into custody.[37]

Just north of Archer Avenue and past Big Jim Colisimo's restaurant on Armour Street stood another popular Chinese brothel in the Levee district. The Shanghai was a three-story brick building run by Madame

Julie, who specialized in "sloe-eyed oriental beauties." The brothel caught the attention of the famous Everleigh sisters Minna and Ada. The sisters successfully bartered for one of the Shanghai's most successful working girls, known as Suzy Poon Tang. Legend has it Suzy began her trade at an early age in Shanghai, China, and later traveled to Singapore and Hong Kong. She later moved to Macao, where she partnered with an English-speaking brothel keeper and learned how to properly prepare an opium pipe for a customer.

Suzy came to the United States, settling in Chicago's red-light district. Minna and Ada learned of Suzy's success and beauty and enticed her to work at their Everleigh club, which, by brothel standards, was much more exquisite than the Shanghai. With Madame Julia's permission, in a fair trade, Suzy moved into the Everleigh. However, she didn't last long before a smitten and well-paying customer swept her away and married the beautiful Suzy.[38]

Another one of Chow Tai's brothels was raided by Chicago police in the spring of 1892. Police searching the less-than-elegant quarters at 166 South Custom House found three women, highly intoxicated on opium, and a man named Sing Moy, whom they determined to be the proprietor. Chow Tai bailed out all four subjects. According to police reports, officers returned to the scene of the raid to find one of the women back on scene, smoking the same pipe to finish the opium the police had interrupted her in consuming.[39]

The Chicago Police Department sent sworn policewomen undercover into a saloon at 223 West Twenty-Third Street owned by Tom Lee. In what was an innovative law enforcement operation for its time, the women entered the tavern and ordered beers. Tom Lee approached the women, whom he assumed were prostitutes, and offered to find the women "escorts."[40] Tom Lee was arrested and was later fined ten dollars in court.

Gambling was already a prominent vice in Chicago, and with the Chinese came their own games of chance. Hidden gambling rooms dotted early Chinatown. Fan Tan was among the more popular illegal games. Fan Tan was a board game of chance. Early on, players used beans as markers, while a Tan Kun, who was essentially the dealer, used a bamboo stick to count the objects. Next to the dealer stood the Ho Kun, who acted as a pit boss and cashier with whom a gambler placed his bets.

Many gambling rooms also sponsored Bung Loo, or simply Loo, which was similar to the old policy games or private lotteries. It was sometimes called a "fishbowl" game. Lottery tickets were placed into a large glass bowl and drawn at random. The winner matched his ticket with one drawn from the fishbowl, much like a typical raffle. Less popular was the game that African American gamblers later introduced as the policy wheel, which was exactly what it sounded like: a large wheel of numbers spun to choose numbers at random. Gamblers occasionally crossed ethnic barriers to try their luck. White and African American gamblers were permitted inside a few of the Chinatown gambling dens; however, the more strict, higher-stakes games were typically Chinese only.

Another popular game of chance was the Bah-ka-pon, or the Chinese Lottery, which was another game very similar to the policy games known throughout much of the city. The difference was that the game did not rely on numbers but rather individual characters to determine a winner. For anywhere between ten cents to five dollars, players were allowed to choose between eighty different characters, written on small slips of yellow paper. The characters included "heaven and earth," "fishes swim," "birds" and "the world is vast," among others.[41] It was said that a gambler improved his chances if he happened to have dreamed about the character the night before the draw. Twenty slips were then chosen at random, crossed and laid out. The gambler with three characters chosen broke even. Five characters paid out double, and a lucky gambler who guessed ten correct characters won two hundred times his original wager. This, of course, was a rare occurrence.

After the police raided one gambling den featuring both Fan Tan and Bung Loo games, Chow Tai came to the defense of the arrested Chinese men. Eleven men total had been arrested at 323 South Clark Street, including the proprietor, Charlie Moy. They were bonded out by Chow Tai and were to appear in court on the tenth of August 1891. Cook County judge Glennon heard from prosecuting witness Tom Kee, who told the court he had led police to the raid after losing fifteen dollars while gambling. The officers testified to their account of the raid, but in the end, Justice Glennon found the defendants not guilty. He felt the officers could not prove that the games were, in fact, a form of gambling. Chow Tai told reporters that the entire incident had been misrepresented and that the laundrymen were simply having a picnic.[42]

Mahjong was one of those games that was once restricted to Chinese players only. The combination of old traditions, coupled with the fact that it was a very difficult game to learn, kept outsiders away. That changed around the beginning of the twentieth century, when gamblers of different races became interested in this exotic and ancient game. The game was played with colorful tiles, shaped much like dominoes but with Chinese characters instead of pips. A pair of dice was also used to determine chance, and a

What's left of the "old" Chinatown neighborhood. *Photograph by author.*

player held his tiles on a rack comparable to the kind used in a Scrabble game. The game was completed in sixteen rounds, and there were many opportunities to gamble side bets, accumulate points and play the odds. The game grew in popularity among outsiders, and for a time, it was denounced by evangelicals as a gateway to immoral behavior.

The gambling houses, brothels and opium dens all needed protection: protection from the police, protection from thieves and protection from rivals.[43] The Moy family of the On Leong Tong was one of the earliest established and most prominent clans in Chinatown affording those protections. The On Leong Tong was said to have evolved from the Chee Kung Tong from China. The Moys enjoyed a monopoly in ruling Chicago's Chinatown underworld, until a young member of the On Leong in New York City named Mock Duck created the rival Hip Sing Tong. The Hip Sing soon gained followers in Chicago.[44]

The first murder in Chicago's Chinatown occurred on the twenty-eighth of August 1882. Ling Dew stabbed Moy Shing Quion in her apartment above 213 West Madison Street in what was described as domestic violence. Ling Ah Yom and Ling Ah Dwe were also arrested as accessories but later found not accountable and released. Lew Ding was found guilty and sentenced to prison, where it was said that he went insane before dying in custody.[45]

Men playing Fan Tan. *Library of Congress, National Archives.*

On a warm August evening in 1887, Chicago police officer Phillip Robinson only had two months on the job when he walked his beat for the last time from the DesPlaines station.[46] He was waved down by two citizens who said they'd been fired on, pointing out the man now fleeing the scene. The officer gave chase and ordered the man to stop near the Sangamon viaduct at Sixteenth Street. Sing Chow Lam fired his pistol three times at the officer, who returned fire and continued his pursuit. The officer was close to catching Lam when Lam turned and fired once more, striking Officer Robinson in the head.

Sing Chow Lam was taken into custody and identified by the weak and dying officer. Lam was said to have been "trembling" while in custody, certain that he would be hanged before trial. Lam also feared that incarceration meant shaving his head, specifically his holy queue, the long braid on the back of his head, without which, according to superstition, one was not allowed into heaven. Officer Robinson expired five days later.

In the ensuing trial, Sing Chow Lam testified on his own behalf. Lam told the judge he did not know the uniformed police officer was an officer of the law and that he had thought Robinson to be part of a group of "hoodlums" and "thugs" who had been harassing him.[47] Lam claimed that he only fired his weapon in self-defense. Sing Chow Lam was acquitted of the murder of Officer Phillip Robinson.

A little over a month after Officer Robinson's murder, the Chicago Police Department conducted coordinated raids of Chinese opium dens and gambling houses. Lieutenant Byrne led the charge with over twenty officers and five patrol wagons in tow. The officers knocked down basement doors to find crowded, dark rooms filled to near suffocation with residue opium smoke. Pipes were dropped and gambling chips, cards and cash money were thrown and scattered as the scenes quickly turned chaotic.[48] Many headed for back-door escapes; others hid under beds and

Exterior view of the Hip Lung Yung Kee & Company storefront in Chinatown, at 233 West Twenty-Second Street, 1920. Chicago Daily News *collection, Chicago History Museum.*

in hallways. Thirty-six Chinese men were arrested inside 322 South Clark Street, another twenty-two men from 295 South Clark Street. In all, over one hundred Chinese men were arrested and taken to the Harrison Street Police Station under arrest.

The officers hadn't finished the arduous process of booking every prisoner when Chow Tai and his partner Wong Sam arrived and offered to bond out one of the elderly arrestees, claiming the man was in poor health. Chow Tai had a controlling interest in the establishment raided at 295 South Clark Street. Chicago police desk sergeant Hogan, being familiar with Chow Tai, agreed to bond out the elder Chinese gentleman. Hogan would later opine to reporters:

> *The Chinese from all over the city come downtown Sunday nights. They go to these resorts and gamble away their money earned during the week at their laundries and to smoke the opium which they buy there at a big profit to the Chinese dealers. They gamble for big stakes too. We often find bills of large denomination mixed in with the chips. Somehow or another there*

> *are five or six Chinamen downtown here, keepers of these places who are getting rapidly rich, just as the big gambling houses always do and the poor "washee washee" Chinaman generally leaves his week's earnings in the place.*[49]

Aside from the outdated, colloquial language that may sound insensitive to today's ear, Sergeant Hogan was correct. Chinese organized crime was on the rise, and much like most ethnic organized crime, the criminals preyed on their own kind.

In 1893, Chicago Police Department sergeant O'Brien and his accompanying patrolman, Officer Glennon, made a grisly discovery in the basement of 328 South Clark Street. It was there they discovered the mutilated body of Jung Din Kan lying next to a bloody hatchet. In a nearby slop sink, Jung Jack Lin was calmly washing his bloody hands and clothes. Sergeant O'Brien promptly arrested Jung Jack Lin and processed him in the nearby Harrison Street Station.

Jung Jack Lin originally denied having committed the murder of his cousin. The defendant told the officers that he had only just arrived from China the evening prior and spent the night with his cousin although they were bitter rivals. Jung Jack Lin said that he left the premises for breakfast, leaving his cousin asleep on a door resting on two chairs as a makeshift bed. Jung Jack Lin told the officers that persons unknown must have snuck in after he left and murdered Jung Din Kan. When he returned from breakfast, he found the victim dead and, in an attempt to wake the deceased, got blood on his hands and clothes. Jung Jack Lin's story did not hold up.[50]

While criminal forensics was still in its infancy, police did notice that the blood on the murder weapon had clotted to such a degree that Jung Jack Lin's timeline of the events was in question, as the murder must have happened much earlier than his breakfast absence. The officers also did not believe that he and his cousin were deadly enemies, as they had slept in one another's presence. Lastly, a footlocker containing valuables belonging to Jung Din Kan had been broken open and its contents pilfered. Jung Jack Lin was charged with first-degree murder.

The case was arraigned and ended up in front of the Honorable Judge Tuthill. The court appointed Chinatown's prominent citizen Sam Moy as an interpreter. During the hearing, Jung Jack Lin's attorney, Sampson, submitted a plea of guilty, possibly hoping for a lenient sentence. Judge Tuthill, wanting to hear Jung Jack Lin's agreement, called Jung Jack Lin to the witness stand, where he was questioned by State's Attorney Pierson. Jung Jack Lin, to the surprise of the court, his interpreter and even his own lawyer, emphatically claimed his innocence, now declaring that he indeed had been in the basement but had not seen the murderer.

Judge Tuthill stopped the proceeding, which had clearly gone awry. State's Attorney Pierson told the court that the defendant did not understand that he was under obligation to tell the truth and that he was not conscious of the nature of U.S. court methods. Pierson observed that in Jung Jack Lin's native country, giving a false testimony could result in torture and/or death. He insisted that Jung Jack Lin be sworn in under the regular oath of the Chinese courts. Judge Tuthill allowed it, and Sam Moy began to swear in Jung Jack Lin, whose demeanor changed drastically. Court reporters described Jung Jack Lin as wild-eyed, "twisting in his seat in agony as he listened to the Chinese oath with a look of deathly fear."[51]

After Sam Moy finished administering the oath, Judge Tuthill once again asked to hear from Jung Jack Lin. State's Attorney Pierson had barely finished the first question when Jung Jack Lin blurted out that he did it. In open court, Jung Jack Lin admitted to killing Jung Din Kan with a hatchet.[52]

Sam Moy later told the press that this was a simple case of larceny gone awry, noting there was tampering with the victim's property.

The press and public listened to Sam Moy because he was considered the unofficial mayor of Chinatown. In broader circles, he was known as the King of the Celestials. Sam emigrated from central China as a teenager in the late 1870s. After landing in San Francisco, he became an accomplished chef employed in an upscale hotel restaurant. Sam would later credit his father for teaching him his traditional cooking skills.[53]

Author's rendering of Sam Moy. *Harrison Fillmore.*

Sam Moy escaped San Francisco in the midst of a violent movement against Chinese immigrants. He saved enough money to travel east to Chicago, where the word was that the Chinese people were more welcome. His timing was impeccable, as there was a sudden craze over chop suey and other Chinese delicacies. He opened a restaurant on Clark Street in the center of Chicago's Chinatown. Soon after, Sam Moy ditched his traditional garb and began to wear Western clothing. Sam was known for being neatly dressed in public. He wore a shirt and tie with a coat and a hat that one newspaper called a "Clark Street hat."[54] Sam was also known for his choice in shoes, which were always the brightest of yellows.[55]

The success of Sam's restaurant, along with his ability to speak nearly perfect English, afforded him power. Sam's association with the On Leong Tong soon made him every immigrant's go-to for problems that arose. He served as a mediator of sorts, not only among his fellow immigrants but also among the "whites" when needed.

The dark side of Sam's rise to power was the opium trade, which festered in the backrooms and basements of Chinatown. Sam, whose real name was Moy Dong Hoy, had two brothers, Moy Dong Chew, otherwise known as Hip Lung, and his youngest brother, Moy Dong Yee. Moy Dong Chew became known in Chicago as Opium Dong.[56] A great majority of the opium smuggled, distributed and sold in Chinatown was from Sam's brother. Opium Dong opened up the Hip Lung Ying Kee company, a front for his drug-smuggling operation. He and Sam also owned several laundries along Clark Street.

Moy Dong Lee was known as a playboy of sorts. He spent half of his time in Hong Kong, acting as the brothers' liaison in the old country. He was fond of fancy cars and riding horseback. Moy Dong Lee spoke fluent English, German and Chinese, and it was his opium connections to the Chinese mainland that funded the On Leong Tong. Moy Dong Lee also created the Hip Lung society in San Francisco, which was the Moy family's way to keep in touch with the organized criminal power in the city with the largest Chinese population in the country.[57]

Sam and his brothers had a controlling interest in most of the gambling and prostitution that occurred in Chinatown. Sam associated with several notorious Chicago underworld figures and was soon recognized as the de facto leader of the Hongmen, which began as a group of unorganized gangsters and highbinders without a clear structure. Sam would go on to lead the Chinese Freemasons, which was a well-organized criminal conglomerate of several tongs. As more Chinese arrived, Freemasons began to split into their respective tongs, including On Leong and Hip Sing. Soon, Sam became the Godfather of Chinatown by leading the biggest tong in the city, the Moy family's On Leong Tong.

The Hip Sing Tong, not nearly as powerful in Chicago, became the primary rival to the On Leong Tong in the late 1800s. The Chinatown sections in the cities of San Francisco, New York and even Seattle saw tong wars rage between the two opposing factions.[58] Yet in Chicago, Sam Moy,

The Hip Lung Yung Kee & Company storefront in Chinatown, at 223 West Twenty-Second Street, 1918. Chicago Daily News *collection, Chicago History Museum.*

as the unofficial mayor of Chinatown, was credited with keeping the peace between the two.

Chinese gangsters were known as highbinders, a name coined in the San Francisco press. The term "highbinder" became synonymous with Chinese gangsters in San Francisco in the late 1800s during the tong wars. Chicago was introduced to the term shortly thereafter as the Hip Sing and On Leong Tong conflict brewed.

Chicago author Richard Lindberg compares Sam Moy to Chicago's Outfit boss John Torrio.[59] This is an appropriate comparison, as Torrio was a quiet, unassuming but dangerous gentleman who ran the Chicago mafia just before Al Capone's reign. On his surface, Torrio, like Sam Moy, was poised and professional. However, Torrio, like Sam Moy, was responsible for running some of the most wicked and violent vice rackets in Chicago. Prostitution, opium use and gambling ran rampant in Chicago's Chinatown, and Sam Moy got a piece of most of it.

Photograph of Chinese miners in Idaho Springs by Dr. James Underhill. *Courtesy of Denver Library Digital Collections.*

Having found legal success in Chicago, Sam Moy was summoned across the country to act as an interpreter. His cases weren't all criminal. At times, he was called to mediate between the Chinese community and their respective political leaders.

A contentious and potentially volatile coal miners' strike was brewing in Braidwood, Illinois. The coal mine threatened to lay off the miners and hire Chinese labor, specifically from Chicago. Sam Moy and the On Leong Association intervened and stopped any Chinese from working as strikebreakers. He was quoted in the *Chicago Tribune*: "Those miners are crazy and we will not send our countrymen up there to be murdered."[60]

In another incident, a woman's jewels were stolen by a Chinese laundryman, who also happened to be in her Bible study group. She filled out a police report but didn't get very far without any evidence, and the police were unable to solve the crime. Chicago police captain James McWeeney turned to Sam Moy. Sam sprang into action. Knowing that the crime could hurt other laundry businesses and in an attempt to hold Chicago's Chinese citizens in high esteem, he gave the suspected crook one hour to return the jewels, no questions asked. The jewels were returned by the thief, Chow

Fook, before the hour was up. According to newspaper accounts, the victim, Mrs. Mooney, was in "painful doubt whether Fook's conscience or threats of death by a thousand cuts used by Moy had the most influence on the obdurate laundryman."[61]

The police turned to Sam Moy for problems big and small. After two local businessmen, Ah Hong and Hong Sing, were arrested for defrauding an insurance company, their tong put up public notices offering a $500 reward for the murders of the two lead detectives, Crowe and Connelly. Chicago Police Department deputy Chief Kipley sat down with Sam Moy and his business partner and brother Hip Lung and explained how he would hold both of them responsible for the murders of his men. Sam Moy intervened, and the contract was quashed.[62]

A gambling dispute arose in which Lee Fong accused Ging Lem of cheating him out of $1,300 in a game. Lee Fong was so incensed that he proceeded to beat Ging Lem about his head with the butt of his pistol. Chicago police arrested Lee Fong but allowed Sam Moy to bail him out. Sam Moy then held his own arraignment in the "Chinese Court," described as an informal trial in which if they, the "Chinese," were able to come to an agreement, the case would be allowed to settle outside of Illinois's criminal court system. If an agreement was not met, the case was "turned over to the regular justice mills."[63]

Sam wasn't only litigating others' problems. In 1892, he found himself in trouble, arrested federally by customs officials for his role in smuggling seven Chinese nationals from Canada into Detroit. Sam also had problems with the U.S. Department of Revenue as it poked around his finances earned through opium, gambling and prostitution.[64]

Federal agents were contacted by a laundry worker named Lem Aut, who reported a massive scandal of false identities and immigration fraud in the heart of Chinatown. Dozens of Chinese nationals were arrested. Sam Moy used his power and influence to ostracize the man from the entire Chinatown community. Soon, Sam's brothers and Chow Tai were assisting in what would become an entire neighborhood's boycott of one man. Under the pressure from his own community, Lem Aut ceased to cooperate with authorities, and the federal government dropped every case.[65]

When the Swedish immigrants began to open local laundries, Sam Moy again organized the Chinatown residents. In what the *Chicago Tribune* coined the "War of the Washtubs," Sam Moy led a boycott of the "Swede" laundries that charged only four cents a shirt, undercutting the Chinese

The first murder in Chicago's Chinatown to cross civilian racial lines occurred on the twenty-sixth of September 1894. A man named Israel Weinberg entered the laundry at 500 South Jefferson Street and demanded his shirts, which had been dropped off some time ago. Yon King did not care for the tone of Weinberg's voice and rudely told him that his shirts were not ready. Weinberg took exception to the delay and began to argue with King. H. Rubenstein was also in the laundry, patiently awaiting his turn, and later told police that as Weinberg exited the store, Yon King took up a hatchet, chased him to the door and struck him in the back. Weinberg, with a hatchet lodged in his back, ran out into the street screaming, attracting passersby and Good Samaritans alike. Yon King began to slash at the crowd at large. He was pelted with rocks and bricks, forcing his retreat back into the laundry. By now, a large crowd had gathered. They pelted the laundry business with rocks and stones until the windows were all shattered. The Chinese men within used the broken glass as projectiles, throwing pieces into the crowd, striking both boys and men. Ah Sing exited the laundry armed with a flatiron. He rushed into the crowd and struck several men, knocking them down to the pavement. At the same time, Sam Sing came out of the laundry with a long-bladed, two-edged knife. He slashed and stabbed at the crowd, wounding several men in the process, until he reached the corner of Wilson and Jefferson, where he met Jacob Boblovsky, who had taken no part in the row and was walking down the street. Sam Sing stabbed Jacob Boblovsky without provocation, plunging the knife deep into his sides several times in quick succession. The police arrived and took the three men into custody.*

Chinatown authorities were quick to come to the aid of all three defendants, and the court records show a Chinese interpreter's version of the defendants' statement in which all three men admitted to committing the crime. The interpreter introduced the defendants as "friends" and stated, "In them is righteousness but little education. The white man scoffed at them, calling them dogs and sons of dogs,

* Marrow and Carter, *In Pursuit of Crime*, 212.

there was not in them the training and education which should teach them to hold their anger within themselves." Cook County judge Gibbons found all three defendants not guilty, and they were acquitted of all charges.*

* "Two Wild Chinamen Run Amok," *Chicago Tribune*, September 28, 1893.

practice of charging ten cents a shirt.[66] Sam was successful in his efforts after the Swedish population moved farther north in the city, saving his ownership interest in several laundries.

Sam Moy may have been the unofficial mayor of Chinatown, but even he had enemies.

CHAPTER 5

RIVALRY

道不同，不相为谋

“Men of Different Principles, Don’t Work Well Together”

Wong Chin Foo—or King Foo, as he was known—was the archnemesis of Sam Moy. King Foo was the outspoken leader of the Chin family and later the Hip Sing Tong. He spent years traveling the country and was an activist for Chinese rights in the United States. King Foo profited from the Hip Sing–controlled opium dens, gambling and prostitution and held an uneasy alliance with African American policy king and Chicago’s first black gangster John “Mushmouth” Johnson.[67]

King Foo called himself a Confucian missionary, and he founded the Chinese Equal Rights League. King Foo stood up to the anti-Chinese movements led by the likes of Denis Kearney, the outspoken anti-immigration and anti-Chinese president of California’s Workingman’s Party. Kearney called the Chinese immigrants “coolies,” a derogatory term the newspapers of the day were all too keen on printing.[68]

The Wong faction of the Six Companies Triad was founded by King Foo as a rival to the Moy family. The Chin family threw its support behind the Wong faction before breaking off to join the Hip Sing Tong.

The Hip Sing/On Leong rivalry story is one of fact blurred with legend. It is said that a Hip Sing emissary from New York City wandered into

Illustration of Wong Chin Foo from *Harper's Weekly*, May 26, 1877.

town and stopped at a shop in Chinatown. Pleased to see his countrymen, he began to tell the shop owner of the purpose of his visit to Chicago. The man related that he was in town to start the Chicago branch of the Hip Sing Tong, with blessings from tongs in San Francisco to New York City. He brought with him ceremonial banners and flyers to distribute. He was to begin the recruitment process immediately and wished to join forces with Chicago's Chinatown population.

The man's mistake was that he had accidentally entered an establishment run by the greater Moy family, loyal to the On Leong. The shopkeeper summoned his friends and brothers, who didn't take kindly to the idea of another organization taking over one they had built up over the years. The man, affiliated with the Chin family, was beaten and his wares stolen, and thus began the long rivalry between the Chin family's Hip Sings and the Moy family's On Leong.

Ching Dak was a frequent gambler in Sam's establishments. His game of choice was Bung Loo. For reasons known only to Ching Dak, he terminated his alliance with the Moy family and instead took up with their rivals, the Hip Sing Tong. On a cold January day, Ching Dak and two associates arrived at the front doors of the Hip Lung grocery on South Clark Street, where Ching Dak was immediately confronted by men loyal to the Moys and the On Leong Tong. The men accused Dak of swearing out warrants for raids of and arrests in establishments backed by the On Leong Tong and the Moys themselves, an accusation Dak denied. The confrontation turned physical with no less than a dozen combatants fighting in the streets. Ching Dak took the brunt of the punishment. It was said that "there was not more than two or three square inches of skin left on his face and the little that remained was black and blue. They knocked him down and rolled him in the mud, kicked him in the face and stomach, and scratched him with their fingernails."[69]

King Foo used this bitter rivalry to his advantage. Nationally, he continued to travel and speak out on the injustices suffered by Chinese Americans, even comparing their plight to that of African American slaves. Meanwhile, he continued profiting from his Hip Sing interests in opium and gambling.

The Chinese Village and Theatre at the World's Columbian Exposition. *Chicago History Museum, National Archives, 1893.*

The four-hundred-year anniversary of Columbus's arrival to the New World was to be celebrated in Chicago during the World's Columbian Exposition. The Moy and Chin families competed to secure a place within the walls of the White City, specifically to build a traditional Chinese teahouse to attract tourists. The Moy family lost their bid to the Wong/Chin families, further simmering the bitter rivalry. The Moy brothers built a large building just outside the grounds of the fair and planned on using it as a Chinese tourist attraction. They sponsored over 250 Chinese tea servers, cooks, dancers and acrobats to perform.[70]

By this time, King Foo had many powerful allies in the federal government. He had served for a time as a customs officer, even after being investigated for opium trafficking by the same government agency just years prior. The Moys' building was never built to code and was not allowed to open. Immigration officials also found that the immigrants the Moy brothers brought over were using false and forged documents. The Moy family lost tens of thousands of dollars on the failed venture, and the rivalry between the two factions continued to boil.

On March 29, 1893, a young Northwestern University student from China named Wong Aloy was enjoying all Chinatown had to offer on South Clark Street. Guilty by his association with King Foo, he was attacked by two members of the Moy family organization, beaten badly but left alive. Police officers arrested Moy Toi Nye and Ung Yok for the brutal attack. The Moy brothers put up $8,000 for the pair: $2,000 for the jail bond and the rest for a defense attorney.[71]

Wong Aloy went into hiding to recover out of the public eye, but King Foo came back into town to act as a voice for what he perceived to be the wrongly persecuted Wongs. He accused the prosecutor's office of being biased toward his family while favoring the Moys—this even after the state's attorney representative, John B. Strassburger, took Wong Aloy into his own home, where he remained bedridden, recovering from the attack. King Foo was quoted as saying that he believed his family "cannot obtain justice through [State's Attorney] Mr Kern in the case of Wong Aloy."[72]

State's Attorney Kern publicly accused King Foo of coming back to Chicago only to disrupt the peace:

> *In my opinion Wong Chin Foo is an adventurer. He came to Chicago at this time, I think, for the purpose of stirring up a quarrel among the Chinamen that he might reap benefit from it....I think I understand Chinamen thoroughly, and believing that Wong Chin Foo had come here to create trouble in Chinatown, I thought the surest way of averting it would be to read the riot act on him. I told Wong Chin Foo that if it had been a white man in the case he would have been fined $25 and the case disposed of long ago. They are making a trivial matter the excuse for a bitter factional fight.*[73]

King Foo responded and repeated his accusation: "It is impossible for any Chinaman in Chicago who is not friendly to the Moy family to obtain justice."[74]

Continuing with his international exploits, King Foo was arrested in New York City for voter registrations fraud. He assisted in solving a murder case in Canada, opened a Chinese theater in Manhattan and was awarded franchise rights to open a Chinese exhibit in Omaha, Nebraska. Eventually, King Foo returned to Chicago, created the Chinese Revolutionary Junta and opened the Confucian Temple. King Foo traveled back to Hong Kong and applied for a passport with the United States consulate to return to the United States but was denied.[75]

In 1898, Wong Chin Foo—King Foo—died after attending a family reunion in his hometown of Shandong. The Moy family syndicate would never again face such a contemptuous adversary.

Four years later, Sam Moy traveled to Milwaukee, Wisconsin, to aid in a murder trial involving Chinese nationals. Sam caught pneumonia and passed away. What followed was a funeral grand enough to be compared to that of any high-profile Chicago gangster.

Sam's body was waked in John Rafferty's Saloon on the corner of Lasalle and Harrison, in the heart of Chinatown. A stage was built to accommodate a procession band honoring Moy's death. According to the *Chicago Inter Ocean*,

> *Chinese flutes screamed shrill, gongs rattled, tom-toms boomed, and Chinese songs all contributed to driving the evil spirit away. Probably no citizen of Chicago ever went to his grave with such a conglomeration of color settings, weird music, discordant noises, and fantastic funeral rites.*[76]

The *Chicago Tribune* reported,

> *The funeral of Sam Moy was the greatest which honored any Chinaman in this country. There were over 175 carriages in line, and a crowd variously estimated at from 2,000 to 10,000 people surged about the grave. At the north end of it was a sort of canopy, and under the casket was placed a roast whole pig, a whole lamb, and many bowls of stewed duck, chicken, and rice, the latter gilded, grain by grain.*[77]

The Hung Society adorned Sam Moy's coffin with peacock feathers, flowers and silk for a procession of over one hundred horse-drawn carriages that escorted his remains to Rosehill Cemetery on the far north side.[78]

CHAPTER 6
VIOLENCE ERUPTS

杀人不眨眼

"KILLING, WITHOUT BLINKING AN EYE"

Sam Moy's brother, Moy Dong Chew, better known as Hip Lung, or Opium Dong, was quick to fill the shoes of his deceased brother, soon becoming recognized as the new mayor of Chinatown. Opium Dong never had the political prowess his brother possessed. While Sam was affable and friendly, Hip Lung was much more subdued and impersonal. Hip Lung also did not have the legal skills or intelligence his brother had and was viewed by most as more of a Chinese gangster and highbinder. In fact, whereas Sam enjoyed praise from high-ranking members of the Chicago Police Department, they had this to say in regard to Opium Dong: "All good Chinese should do all in their power to rid the world of such a man."[79]

But Opium Dong was comfortable in his adopted city. Despite his brushes with the law and the anti-Chinese sentiment growing in the United States, he was quoted as saying,

> [The residents of Chicago] *never said to me that the Chinese have got the perfection of crimes of four thousand years. They never asked me whether or not I ate rats or snakes. They seemed to believe that we had souls to save and these souls were worth saving. The Chicagoans found us a peculiar people, to be sure, but they liked to mix with us.*[80]

In an interview with a *Chicago Tribune* reporter, Opium Dong admitted to owning more laundry shops than he could handle. The reporter pressed him, asking specifically about opium consumption. Opium Dong swiftly denied having any knowledge of this. He then accused the reporter of telling lies and forced the newsman off his premises. The reporter followed up and interviewed a local Chinese man who admitted that Opium Dong was certainly the richest man in Chicago's Chinatown and possibly all the Chinatowns in the nation. The man referred to the Hip Lung grocery as an employment service, saying all Chinese men seeking a job began there. The man admitted that often, the Chinese workers were not paid in wages but rather in food and opium. The article finished with a quote from Chicago police captain Bartram. After acknowledging that Opium Dong and his people would always find justice and protection from the police department, he stated, "It's true they smoke opium and gamble at Hip's place, but we have more important things to look out for than the Chinamen. Crime has been lessened on the south side. Instead of raiding harmless Chinese joints we are catching thieves and preventing crime."[81]

Author's rendering of Moy Dong Chew, aka "Opium Dong." *Harrison Fillmore.*

Chicago's Chinatown had two baseball teams, thanks to Opium Dong. In an attempt to assimilate into the local culture, he invited the public and the press to watch baseball games between the Clark Street Nine and the Wabash Avenue Nine. According to one press account, there were a couple of beat cops on scene, who, after admitting the game was against ordinance, permitted play anyway.[82] The games followed most of the American rules, although there was apparently no strike count: one could swing away until exhaustion. And dirty tricks were encouraged, such as shoving a runner off base to tag them out. All in all, most thought that the games were good fun and good publicity for Opium Dong and Chinatown.

The *Chicago Tribune* reported the score on one of the games, naming the Clark Street Nine victors with twenty-six runs, beating the Wabash Team with only four. The newspaper related that after the game, the players consumed generous amounts of beer and tea and that the winning team

Top: Illustration of the Hip Lung Store. *Artist unknown, circa 1880s.*

Bottom: Illustration of the Hip Lung Restaurant. *Artist unknown, circa 1880s.*

had won a wager for a barrel of rice and five pounds of opium.[83]

Despite the good publicity, the Chin family did not honor Opium Dong's rank within the Chinatown neighborhood. They did not honor any of the Moy family members or their associates. Disputes over territory and money had sparked recent violence between the two competing criminal organizations.

On October 18, 1908, Chin Wai was murdered in front of Kenna's saloon after refusing to join the Moys' On Leong Tong. He was executed at close range, shot fourteen times. Responding police officers found Harry Lee hiding near the crime scene, and he was arrested. However, Opium Dong and his brother Moy Dong Lloy would soon face charges of conspiracy to murder after the state's attorney found them and their On Leong Tong responsible.[84]

During the ensuing trial, Chicago was formally introduced to the Chinese tong rivalry. The *Chicago Tribune* reported that the courtroom was filled, split in half with the Chin family and associated Hip Sings on the prosecutor's side and the Moy family and the On Leong Tong on the defendants' side of the courtroom.[85]

The prosecution asserted that Harry Lee was hired by Opium Dong to murder Chin Wai. However, Louis Cohen, a bystander and witness to the murder, did not implicate Harry and instead described how

> *a heavyset Chinaman dressed in oriental garb, approached him* [Chin Wai] *and drew a revolver, firing at Chin Wai's breast when about three feet away. Chin threw up his hands, and as he whirled around on his heels another shot was fired. The wounded Chinaman fell on his back. And the murderer, standing directly over him, emptied the one revolver into his body,*

South Dearborn Street in the Levee district. *Originally published by Clifford G. Roe in* The Great War on White Slavery, *1911.*

> *threw away the gun, and, drawing another, fired several more shots at the prostrate man. Then he turned and ran.*[86]

The case included testimony involving the On Leong's soon-to-be-constant thorn in their side, Chin Jack Lem. A witness told jurists that the Moy brothers had offered him and Lem $600 for every Hip Sing member they murdered. The conversation took place in the basement of the Hip Lung grocery, Opium Dong's legitimate front for his larger gambling establishment. The witness said he was offered protection within the store after the deed was done and that if the police did catch anyone, they would be provided legal representation and $30 a month in the event of prosecution. Opium Dong also offered $1,000 to be sent back to family in China should the assassins themselves be killed.[87]

After five hours of jury deliberations, the defendants were acquitted. Opium Dong held a grand banquet in his own honor at the Shanghai restaurant in the heart of Chinatown. He served over three hundred guests at fifteen dollars a plate. The feast was an opulent event, lasting over three hours as course after course was brought out to the guests. The champagne was on the house and flowing. In attendance were nine of the twelve jurors, and although both presiding judge Chytraus and prosecuting attorney Popham were invited, they both failed to attend, much to Opium Dong's regret.[88]

Chinese City Hall Building (On Leong Merchants Association), Chicago, Illinois, 1928. Chicago Sun-Times/Chicago Daily News *collection, Chicago History Museum.*

View of Clark Street north from Harrison Street in the Loop community area of Chicago, Illinois. Chicago Daily News *collection, Chicago History Museum.*

Opium Dong's control over Chicago's Chinatown began to grow.

Chicago was expanding. The population was growing, and the residential areas were spreading outward from the lake. Around this time, a "new" Chinatown was proposed. Construction was to begin south of Twenty-Second Street on new buildings and infrastructure as the current Chinatown was becoming crowded and a new push to create a business-centered downtown emerged.

The Moy family embraced the move. They saw an opportunity for growth and expansion but also one for peace. In an agreement that came during a National Declaration of Peace between tongs nationwide, the Hip Sing Tong would keep all of the current Chinatown territory, while the On Leong Tong would move into "new" Chinatown.

On its surface, the On Leong Tong's move south of Twenty-Second Street had the appearance of the gang being run out of Chinatown by its rivals. However, the move turned out to be very profitable and gave the criminal organization even more power. While the move originally brought peace to the Chinese community, the power struggle grew, as did the influence of the On Leong Tong.

Ninyang Huigan was a gambler and money lender who challenged the Moy family for power. Around the same time, Chin Jack Lem, a gambler who straddled his alliances with both the Hip Sing and On Leong, attempted to branch out on his own and begin his own gambling empire.[89] The On Leong Tong leadership reacted to his actions at a national meeting in Pittsburgh where he was officially thrown out of the On Leong society for good. After weathering Ninyang Huigan's attempted coup and defeating the Hip Sing leadership, Opium Dong and the Moys tightened their grip on Chicago's Chinatown.

The On Leong Tong began to recruit. Specifically, they began to demand that gamblers, pimps and opium peddlers join their organization and pay dues. Those who refused were met with violent consequences.

CHAPTER 7

TONG WAR

以毒攻毒

"FIGHT POISON WITH POISON"

The growing influence of the On Leong Tong and their strongarm tactics created a violent conflict as the Hip Sing Tong actively resisted their attempts to take over Chicago's Chinatown for good.

On a cold December evening in 1909, tension between the two rival factions came to a head at 333 South Clark Street. A large group of Hip Sing fought on the street with an equally large group of On Leong members. They fought with fists and feet and then bricks and bats. Hip Sing member Wong Fong, aka "Jumbo," fearing his side was losing, pulled out a pistol in the center of the fracas and shot On Leong Tong member Sing Moy dead.[90]

The police were already converging on the area when the shots were fired. Immediately, a total of ten Hip Sing Tong members were arrested. Wong Jumbo Fong was charged with the murder, while the other nine faced accessory charges. The group was held in custody until the following February, when a grand jury, on learning that the murder was a result of a large disturbance and violent clash, decided there was not enough evidence to prosecute any of the offenders.

The Chicago Police Department responded to the violence with frequent raids. In one incident, they arrested thirty Chinese Chicagoans, citing that in doing so, they hoped to prevent the outbreak of a tong war. Their efforts proved fruitless, as the war continued for many years.

On the twenty-second of April, Hip Sing member Jung Sing was killed at 509 South Clark Street. During the wild shootout, bystander Charles Erickson was struck with an errant round. Detectives later discovered On Leong Tong member Charles Lee had been sent from the city of Pittsburgh for the hit. The outsider was proof of the tongs' organization on a national level and became historical proof of Chicago's Chinatown tongs' willingness to hire muscle from other cities, provided they were members and loyal to the tong.[91]

On the tenth of June 1912, another Moy family member was gunned down. On Leong associate Mow Tong Moy was murdered in the streets. Police later claimed it was a case of mistaken identity.[92]

The mistaken identity motive didn't quite hold water. Weeks later, Hip Sing member Chun Mock was murdered by Harry Eng Hong. After being positively identified, Hong fled to Boston's Chinatown, where he assumed a new identity. It would take detectives two years to locate, arrest and charge the offender.

In 1914, Chin Yen was found with his head bashed in by bricks in the alley behind his laundry business at 226 West Twenty-Second Street. An associate of Yen named George Coo ran to his aid, firing a handgun at the offenders, who fled through the opposite end of the alley. No arrests were ever made.[93]

One year later, the rival tongs proved that the violence wasn't contained to merely Chinatown. On the near northwest side of Chicago, Chang "Frank" Lee was murdered by Lee Fook Chang. Frank was found outside of his laundry business at Madison and Kedzie, shot and hacked to death by a cleaver or hatchet. Chang was charged and sentenced to prison.[94]

The On Leong and Hip Sing Tongs came to a peace agreement. The world was engaged in the Great War, and the nation's Chinatowns became quiet, including Chicago's. The neighborhood would enjoy several years of a tenuous treaty.

On the thirteenth of January 1921, Hip Sing member Yuen Good Tong was found dead in the basement of 431 South Clark Street in the heart of Chinatown, beneath the Sam Lung & Co. Grocery, controlled by the On Leong. He was shot once in the back. Police suspected that the Hip Sing member was lured to the basement and killed as revenge for the murder of On Leong member Chang "Frank" Lee. A day later, police arrested four On Leong members, Yat Lee, John Lee, Hong Kune and Chuck Hong Toy. A week after that, Hip Sing members Hong Way and Chin Jing were arrested after a coroner's inquest charged them both as accessories. Three months later, all the defendants were released as the prosecution could not meet their burden of proof.[95]

One of the earliest murders in Chicago's Chinatown to gain national attention was that of respected Chinese businessman Lo Sing Sun, otherwise known as Charlie Sing. Charlie, who was an honored and ranking member in the On Leong Tong, was found stabbed to death on the front porch of his home on Archer Avenue. He had a stab wound behind his right ear, several on his scalp and one in his chest and two wounds in his neck, which had severed his carotid artery.

The police originally suspected Charlie was a victim of the On Leong and Hip Sing rivalry—that is, until they entered his home to find the place in disarray, spattered in blood. Police noted naked bloody footprints, Chinese sandal prints and prints made by a large-sized, American-made shoe. They also found Charlie's bewildered wife, lying in a pool of blood that was not her own, clearly under the heavy influence of opium.

Alice Sing, Charlie Sing's wife, was the daughter of Missouri farm folk. She told police that they had both been sleeping when two Chinese gunmen entered their bedroom. They threw a hood over her head, and, she claimed, she blacked out. "Charlie knew too much," according to Annie, and he was killed by hatchetmen because of his connections to the On Leong underworld.

Frank Moy, of the Moy clan, who was now considered the new mayor of Chinatown, arrived on the crime scene. Frank opined on a motive: "Maybe money, maybe revenge, maybe something else." Frank then offered a healthy reward to anyone who captured Charlie's killers.

The police began to unravel the complicated events leading up to Charlie's murder. Annie had been enjoying the company of George Der Norn. George was part Cantonese and had visited Annie under the premise of bringing her a dress, but the gesture developed into a request to remain at the Sing home for a time. Charlie did not approve, and a Polish servant girl told police that the couple quarreled.

The Chicago police began a manhunt for George Der Norn and raided his room on Clark Street. George was nowhere to be found. However, among his belongings, police found a black book of the Hip Sing Tong with Charlie Sing's name inside.

Famous San Francisco detective Willie Lee inserted himself into the investigation and learned that Charlie had been robbed one month prior to his death. Charlie had also cooperated in the investigation, which was not approved of in Chinatown tongs, and the Chinese suspects were prosecuted.

Charlie Sing's life insurance money went to his brother Sam Sing, who swore to a complaint charging Annie Sing with her husband's murder. A judge found the evidence wholly insufficient and rendered a verdict of not guilty. Charlie's murder has never been solved.*

* Marrow and Carter, *In Pursuit of Crime*, 213.

Detectives from Milwaukee traveled south to Chicago to search for Lok Wok, an alleged On Leong gunman. The Hip Sings had placed a bounty on Lok Wong's head, and a Milwaukee member of the Hip Sing Tong named Wong Tak Go had taken the contract. Detectives believed Lok Wok learned of the contract and snuck into Milwaukee to murder the assassin himself, beating him to the punch.[96]

The On Leong Tong hired assassin Wong Jo Hong to work at the Hip Sing–controlled Madison Square Chop Suey Restaurant. While Hong was employed, gathering intelligence on the Hip Sing, the On Leong Tong made violent plans. In late October 1924, with several witnesses present, Wong Jo Hong and two other gunmen murdered Hip Sing member and part owner Willie Kee Kai in the restaurant's kitchen.[97]

On the same evening, the Hip Sing gunmen were quick to retaliate with acts of violence at several On Leong–associated locations. Suspected tong members entered an On Leong laundry at 810 North Paulina and opened fire. Two members of the Moy family were struck and wounded. Charlie Hung escaped harm after three Hip Sing gunmen shot at him in his laundry at 1631 North Kedzie, and Joe Lee survived an attempt on his life after gunmen fired at him in his chop suey parlor at 4032 North Milwaukee. On the far southeast side, Charles Chong was unscathed after gunmen shot through the windows of his laundry near Eighty-Third Street and Burley. Frank Moy publicly blamed Jack Chin Lem for the violence.[98]

Later that winter, a prominent member of the Moy clan survived a hit by the Hip Sing Tong. Kwong was walking from his import business on Twenty-Second Street to his laundry down the block when two gunmen ran up and began to fire their weapons. He was shot three times in the back, and as his body spun around, a final round entered his chest, barely missing his heart. Kwong collapsed on the street, but responding Chicago police officers captured Hip Sing assassins Wong Way and a young Harry Lee, who would later become a ranking member in the tong. Both men were positively identified by Kwong.[99]

Chicago citizens felt as if their city was under siege from the warring tongs. The Chicago Police Department ramped up patrols in Chinatown and made several arrests of armed members of both tongs. They conducted opium raids and crashed gambling dens, but the pressure did little to tamp down the violence at the time. The *Chicago Tribune* quoted an anonymous captain within the Chicago Police Department, who said, "Our only chance at cleaning up one of these murders is to catch the killer in the act and kill the killer on the spot. Maybe that will stop them. I don't know."[100]

Hip Sing Tong members Tom and Sam Lee ran a gambling room in the basement of the Wing Hing Lung restaurant at 429 South Clark Street. A gambler named Wong Chu had been losing all night. When he lost a $300 bet to Hip Sing Tong member Wong Sai, Chu became incensed and accused Sai of cheating. Sai demanded his money. Chu stood up from his seat and stated, "Well, if I don't pay it, what are you going to do about it?"[101] Sai drew a pistol and fired a shot at Chu, mortally wounding him. Another gambler present, an On Leong Tong member named Joe Wing, also drew a pistol and fired several rounds at Wong Sai, wounding him. Tom and Sam Lee were also wounded.

Such was the story given by Frank Moy, who intervened in the subsequent coroner's inquest. He gave statements to the press that the incident was not the beginning of a new tong war. Moy assured the suspicious reporters that the incident was simply a misunderstanding and that the On Leong member, who was visiting Chicago from Seattle, was merely coming to the aid of the deceased gambler.[102]

Author's rendering of Frank Moy. *Harrison Fillmore.*

Contrary to Frank's explanation, the motive established by police detectives—one that was supported by witnesses—was that Seattle On Leong Tong member Joe Wing was hired to shoot up Tom and Sam Lee's Hip Sing gambling house for not paying tribute to the On Leong. The coroner's inquest later determined Joe Wing to be culpable, and he was charged accordingly.

Frank Moy was the son of Moy Dong Chew, better known as Opium Dong. After his father's brush with the law, Frank came into power. Frank was fond of wearing thick gold chains and expensive suits. He never wore traditional Chinese clothing and drove a brand-new, shiny black Lincoln. A spot in front of the On Leong building was reserved for him. Frank was never shy of the limelight. He was part owner of the Won Kow restaurant and spent most of his time in inner Chinatown, but he lived in a home with his family on the far south side of the city. Frank had a daughter, Rita, who would accompany her father to watch mahjong games in the neighborhood. Frank doted on his daughter, described as a "tomboy" by the press, and she would accompany him often on his Chinatown routes.[103] She even chased down three bandits after being stuck up and robbed on East Forty-Fourth Street.[104]

Chin Jack Lem was gaining prominence within the ranks of the On Leong Tong. However, he proved to be a thorn in the side of the powerful Moy family. Lem was accused of skimming from the street tax he collected and freelancing extortion plots. He was later accused of stealing from the coffers of the On Leong, and the organization began the process of throwing him out altogether. Chin Jack Lem then did the unthinkable and flipped his loyalty to the Hip Sing Tong, assuming a leadership role with his former rivals. The move would incite additional violence between the tongs.

On the second of September 1923, Hip Sing member Chin Ming Shing was found murdered in a bed behind his laundry business near Broadway and Rosedale on the north side of the city. Police found the thirty-five-year-old laundryman with a hatchet lodged in his forehead. A few blocks away, in a second laundry business owned by Chin, they found Sue Ching Chong dead, hanging by the neck. The Cook County coroner's office declared it a murder/suicide.[105]

A few months later, forty-five-year-old William Lee Tai, owner of the Oriental Inn at 4012 North Lincoln Avenue, was found beaten to death in an abandoned brownstone on the second floor of 608 South Federal. The coroner found that Tai had died several days before his body was discovered. Police speculated that he was killed in retaliation for the murder of Hip Sing member Yuen Good Tong.[106]

The On Leong held a national convention in Cleveland in July 1924. Hundreds of members from across the country attended, along with newly elected national secretary William P. Lee, from Chicago. The event was to

Left: Author's rendering of China Jack Lem. *Harrison Fillmore.*

Right: Author's rendering of William P. Lee. *Harrison Fillmore.*

take place in the newly built On Leong Cleveland headquarters on Ontario Street. On his arrival, Lee demanded protection from local law enforcement, noting the presence of several rival Hip Sing Tong members.

William P. Lee was described as American born, educated and professional. He had, for a time, been a correspondent for the *Chicago Daily News*, an experience that made him media savvy. He would host fancy galas, inviting the most prominent politicians and judges in town. He once threw a dinner party for over five hundred people featuring 144 courses of fine delicacies.[107] He was shy neither of the limelight nor the press. He was a voice for immigrants and encouraged the fostering of American ideals. He was in charge of the Twenty-Fourth Precinct and active in the First Ward. He'd even assisted on mayoral campaigns.

The Cleveland police, well aware of their own tong rivalries and associated violent crimes, took heed of Lee's warnings. With William P. Lee's assistance, they began a crackdown on the Hip Sing joints in their city, conducting multiple raids and effecting mass arrests. In all, thirty-one Hip Sing members, many from Chicago, San Francisco and New York City, were arrested. The police also confiscated opium pipes, opium and several revolvers.[108]

The On Leong convention was held as planned, and there were no recorded incidents of rival violence. However, before the celebration ended, William P. Lee once again went to the police for help. The National President of the

On Leong, Wong Sing, had been kidnapped by Chin Jack Lem and eight of his henchmen. Sing was held at gunpoint and forced to sign over $70,000 to their turncoat associate. When Sing refused the first time, witnesses stated that Lem grabbed Sing by the collar, putting the revolver in his face and demanding his signature. Sing signed the deed. Cleveland authorities obtained warrants for the henchmen, who were promptly arrested and charged. But Chin Jack Lem had fled the jurisdiction.

Back in Chicago, William P. Lee began assisting law enforcement. He met with Chicago police sergeants William Bowler and John Howe. The law enforcement men went in disguise with William P. Lee's aid, dressing in traditional Chinese garb. William P. Lee led the officers, who disguised as mandarins, to a shop at 2145 South Archer Avenue. Lem was observed within, snatched up, quickly placed into custody, charged and arraigned in local court. However, Lem managed to make bail and absconded to parts unknown before Cleveland authorities could extradite him.[109] Subsequently, violence between the tongs would erupt nationwide.

Over the next few months, Chicago police recorded two separate shootings between the rival tongs. Both victims survived the attack. But on the eleventh of October, Wong Foon Sing was found at 437 South Clark Street. He had been shot to death in front of his home by an unidentified offender whom witnesses described as Chinese. Wong Foon Sing, who was a member of the Hip Sing, died on the sidewalk. In late October, an explosion rocked Chinatown. An On Leong laundry at 217 West Twenty-Second Place was the site of a tong bombing. Two employees inside the establishment escaped harm, but the attack brought attention to the conflict.[110]

On Christmas Day in 1924, On Leong Tong member Quong Moy was murdered while working in his laundry at 217 West Twenty-Second Street. Police arrested two Hip Sing Tong members, Harry Lee and Wong Way. The charges did not stick, and a coroner's inquest had both defendants stricken from the case. On New Year's Eve, Frank Moy engaged in a gunfight with six rivals, grazing one in the ear. Responding police found Frank armed and wearing a bulletproof vest for his protection, citing the murder of his cousin, Quong Moy.[111]

The On Leong Tong blamed Chin Jack Lem and his exploits for the rash of murders. They also held the Hip Sing Tong accountable because of his flip-flopped allegiance. The Hip Sing Tong disowned Chin Jack Lem and claimed that he had never officially been part of their organization. In several public and newspaper-reported events, the two tongs attempted to make peace.

217 West Twenty-Second Street. *Photograph by author.*

The trial of Lem's henchmen began in December 1924. William P. Lee was in attendance and seemed to be assisting the prosecution in the case. It was reported later that William P. Lee was a little too involved with the prosecution, glad-handing lawyers, police and court personnel while distributing cigars.[112]

While prosecutors presented their case, defense attorneys argued that the men were set up as rivals of an On Leong Tong conspiracy. The defense even found two witnesses who testified that Sing willingly signed over the cash but without reason or motive for doing so. In the end, a jury found all the defendants guilty, and the men were sentenced to prison for terms ranging from two to thirty years.

A few weeks later, Chin Jack Lem was located and arrested in New York City. In the fanfare that followed, Lem told reporters that he was being framed by the On Leong Tong. He presented a bulletproof vest to reporters, which he had taken to wearing in fear for his life.[113] His trial began one month later. William P. Lee was once again front and center.

China Jack Lem's defense began to fall apart in court. A Cleveland detective identified him in court. Lem's former landlord, who had initially provided an alibi, claimed he was bribed into making the statement. According to court reporters, during the trial, an angry Lem lashed out in open court, pointing at William P. Lee in the gallery. "I taught him all he knows, now he turns against me."[114]

Jack Chin Lem was found guilty and sentenced to fifteen years. Shortly after his finding, a new wave of violence shook Chinatowns nationwide.

On February 6, 1925, at nearly two o'clock in the morning, twenty-two-year-old Ow Tong Ock was found stabbed to death in his bed at 936 Airdrie Place, now Gordon Terrace. That same evening, police arrested Joe Ah, Tung Ng, Charlie Jung, Henry Jung, Wong Forn, Chim Tong and George Yep. The defendants were given bonds between $15,000 and $20,000, which were extremely high for the era. The subsequent rulings and motions successfully freed all the defendants but two. George Yep and Joe Ah were sentenced to fourteen years in Joliet prison.[115]

In the summer of 1925, federal agencies began a crackdown in Chicago's Chinatown. Several opium dens were raided, gambling houses were shut down and suspected illegal immigrants were detained. The odd thing about this particular crackdown is that every target was an On Leong establishment. None of the opium dens, brothels or gambling houses were under the Hip Sing Tong's protection. The irregularity, along with the timing of Chin Jack Lem's incarceration, did not go unnoticed.

Lee Way Hoo was a ranking member of the Hip Sing Tong. He had spent the evening at the Mong Sang Share Association building. The association was an employment service but also served as a social club for the Hip Sings. Lee exited the establishment at approximately two o'clock in the morning. A gunman ran up to Lee as he descended the front stairs and opened fire. Lee died on the front stoop of 825 South State Street. On Leong member Lum Gee was arrested for the murder; however, he was later acquitted of the crime.[116]

Two days after Lee Way Hoo's murder, Frank Moy declared that the On Leong Tong and the Hip Sing Tong had signed a declaration of peace.

After peace was declared, the On Leong Tong celebrated by dedicating their newly built, massive headquarters on Wentworth Avenue just south of Twenty-Second Street. The three-story structure nearly took up a whole city block and was ornately decorated in terra cotta with Chinese symbolism. The brick facade included outdoor breezeways and towering traditional Chinese pagodas on the corners. The building was to serve as an informal city hall with several offices, classrooms and a shrine. The complexity of the structure also protected nefarious activities such as secret meetings and gambling.

The peace treaty didn't last very long. On the twenty-third of March 1927, Chin Park, a young member of the On Leong Tong, was found murdered in the backroom of Tom Jack's gambling house at 200 West Twenty-Second Street. Park was shot five times, and three other On Leong members were wounded in the fray; however, none of the wounded cooperated with the subsequent police investigation.[117]

The next morning, Frank Moy was quick to point the finger at the Hip Sing Tong in the press. "The Tong war has opened again and we need special protection as the Hip Sing Tongmen are planning to invade our district." He added, "The Hip Sings have long tried to invade Chicago since moving their headquarters to New York two years ago."[118]

Chicago police lieutenant William Bowler, who was credited with arranging the truce two years before, was questioned by reporters regarding the murder. He was quoted as simply stating, "The war is on."[119]

The very next day, Moy Sing was closing up his laundry business, which was a few miles northwest of Chinatown, at 3206 West Lake Street. Despite being a Moy, Sing was a member of the Hip Sing Tong, and that made him a target. On Leong Tong gunmen Moy Got and Lee Woo Wong rushed into the establishment and opened fire. Bullets tore into Sing, killing him. Sing's eight-year-old son was also shot, though not fatally.

Hip Sing Tong revenge was swift. Only two hours later, Hip Sing gunmen Tommy Jue, Gilbert Lee and Lee Hung walked into a laundry business owned and operated by Frank Moy's cousin, Yukkong "Kong" Moy, near Lake Street and Ashland. Kong was shot several times as the police scrambled from one crime scene to the next.

Police officers returning to the scene of Sing's murder found four armed members of the Hip Sing Tong, apparently on their way to inflict more damage. Their target was never disclosed, but the arrested gunmen did admit to being armed because of the ongoing war.

Chicago's deputy chief of detectives, John Stege, told reporters that the "Hip Sings struck first," breaking the truce agreed on two years earlier.[120] Stege placed the blame for the recent flare-up on a murder that occurred over five years earlier in Los Angeles in which a Hip Sing member was killed by an On Leong tongsman. The Hip Sing Tong demanded a cash payment for "peace," but the On Leong Tong refused. Members of both rival gangs were murdered in cities all over the nation.

In the days that followed, in an attempt to quell the violence, Stege himself spoke to Hip Sing Tong ranking members Wong Lee Hoo, Huie Sing and Chin Foy. He also pleaded with On Leong bosses Tom Jack and Frank Moy to come to some kind of peace agreement.

On the fourteenth of August 1928, Eng Pak, a member of the Hip Sing Tong, was leaving the Toy Den Quay Theater, a Chinese opera house near Twenty-First and Archer. He flagged down a yellow taxicab to take him home. After Pak climbed into the cab, two On Leong hitmen ran up to the vehicle and fired handguns into the car. Eng Pak was killed instantly.[121]

On the fifteenth of October, two Hip Sing Tong gunmen stormed a restaurant owned by Chinee Lee and On Leong Tong member Willie Cook. The tongsmen opened fire, spraying the restaurant with bullets. Willie Cook was shot through his neck and died on the scene. An African American waitress working in the restaurant named Bernice Orshorn was shot in the arm. Vernon Taylor, the African American chef employed by Willie, was also grazed during the shooting.[122] Not unlike the back-to-back vengeful murders in 1927, the Hip Sings were quick to retaliate. On that very same day, a man named Jong Biu Ging was found shot and killed in his laundry business at 1944 West Madison.

That same year, 1928, Moy Dong Chew, otherwise known as Opium Dong, passed away. Opium Dong's lavish funeral was larger than even his brother Sam's services two decades prior. Chinese music echoed along Wentworth Avenue with a procession led by large waving flags and banners. Opium Dong was survived by his son Dong Hoy Moy, who would play an important role over the next few decades in Chicago's Chinatown.

Another tentative peace treaty was reached between the On Leong and Hip Sing Tongs. Like the treaty before, it didn't last very long. In the summer of 1929, each tong blamed the other for starting the violence. The On

The Guey Sam restaurant on the corner of Twenty-Second Street and Wentworth was one of the most popular in Chinatown. The location was also known for serving some of Chicago's better-known underworld figures, including those in Al Capone's organization. The murder of Frank Moy in front of the place caused much speculation. The victim shared the same name with but was not related to Frank Moy, the "mayor of Chinatown."

The victim was leaving the restaurant when he was accosted by Savaria Cortes and Pasquale Lumetta. Detectives would later determine the motive to be a robbery gone wrong, after Frank Moy was beaten to death. The fact that both offenders, who were arrested and charged, were of Italian descent created rumors and whispers of trouble between the Italian Mafia and the Chinatown tongs. Despite speculation, no other violence was attributed to this possible rivalry.*

* "Moy, Chinese Merchant, Dies from Beating," *Chicago Tribune*, December 3, 1927.

Leong Tong claimed the Hip Sing broke the truce by shooting one of their members, Kar Leong Wong. However, the Hip Sing Tong considered that incident to be retaliation for the murder of one of their members, Yee Sun, who was killed at ten o'clock that same evening. Yee Sun was shot and killed at 2223 South Wentworth by On Leong member Joe Tuck. The exact time of Kar Leong Wong's shooting remained in question.[123]

Another theory for the broken peace agreement was the opening of the Hip Sing Social Club on Wentworth and Twenty-First Street, dangerously close to On Leong territory. Hip Sing Tong leader Lester Lee opened the clubhouse, essentially thumbing his nose at the On Leong Tong's dominance in the "new" Chinatown.[124]

With great fanfare, pomp and circumstance, another peace accord was signed, this time in New York City. On the thirteenth of August, newspapers reported that thirty members of rival tongs, Chicago representatives among them, signed a peace agreement in the offices of Dr. Samuel Sung Young, the Chinese consul general. Newspapers reported that two hours after the signing, two Chinese men were stabbed by rivals in Newark, New Jersey.[125]

October of that year proved particularly violent after Hip Sing Tong member Joe Wai was murdered in the heart of Chinatown. Shortly after that, On Leong Tong member Frank Sing's bullet-riddled body was found behind his laundry business on the south side. On the fourteenth of October, three Chinese men were shot in what appeared to be separate incidents. One man was shot in the neck and another two suffered non-life-threatening injuries. All three survived their attacks. The Chicago Police Department blamed the tong war for the events.[126]

In the early evening hours of the twenty-ninth of December, Jung Kam was found murdered in his laundry business on the north side of the city at 2210 North Western Avenue. He was shot four times. Police were not able to establish a motive.

The Chicago Police Department, partnered with federal authorities, kept the pressure on Chinatown tongs, striking at their illicit businesses. They'd enjoyed some success at cracking down on opium dens in and around Chinatown. The raids were specific and successful, and it became increasingly clear there was an informant cooperating.

On the eighteenth of February, at 1:40 in the morning, Don Yip Poy was murdered on the corner of Twenty-Second Street and Wentworth. A gunman had ambushed him and made good his escape. Federal authorities later revealed that Poy was indeed an undercover informant for the federal government and was specifically investigating the opium trafficking rings in Chicago's Chinatown.[127] The case remains unsolved.

Frank Moy, while intervening in a dispute involving ranking On Leong member Harry Hee, was arrested for carrying a concealed pistol. Frank later claimed that he was "deputized" without detailing exactly when this occurred or by whose authority. The matter came at the same time William P. Lee was reported as missing. Lee, another ranking member in the On Leong, had recently lost a restaurant business investment to receivership, leaving many to wonder what happened to the $57,000 William P. Lee had been given.[128] All three men, ranking members of the On Leong Tong, would play vital roles in the organization for years to come.

Chan Kong Gan was on his way to work in the early hours of the seventh of June 1930. He was walking on the sidewalk near the corner of Waller and Madison on the city's far west side when he was approached by several members of the Hip Sing Tong. The Hip Sing Tong was angry with Chan Kong Gan because he had left the organization just two weeks earlier to become a member of the On Leong. Police were unable to determine which Hip Sing member pulled the trigger, but they arrested Henry Luke, Tom Ying, Albert Young and Joe Took. After an evidentiary hearing, the coroner recommended the arrests of Hip Sing president Lester Lee. Lee

Harry Eng and his uncle John ran the Paradise Inn Chinese restaurant at 4007 West Madison Avenue. They had opened the restaurant two years before, but the business was cutting into the profits of the New Paradise Chinese Restaurant, which had opened eight years earlier, literally around the corner at 18 South Crawford, now Pulaski. The owner of that restaurant, Eng Won, who had ties to the On Leong Tong, had warned Harry Eng that the restaurant was in violation of the "one mile rule,"* an unofficial rule prohibiting Chinese to open up a similar business within the area of an already established business outside of Chinatown.

On a fall night in 1936, a gunman walked into the Paradise Inn looking to kill Harry Eng. Harry wasn't there that evening, and instead, John Eng, Harry's brother, was murdered in front of seven witnesses. After determining the motive, detectives went looking for Eng Won and, after careful witness interrogation, identified Eng King as the assassin.

According to Harry's granddaughter Monica Eng—who, much later, interviewed one of Harry's sons—the surviving restaurateur was approached by the On Leong Tong. He was offered amnesty and protection; he simply had to switch his allegiance from the Hip Sing to the On Leong Tong.†

The Chinatown community became involuntarily engulfed in another murder in the summer of 1935. After her own daughter died from an illness, a woman named Blanche Dunkel had taken in her son-in-law, the widower, named Ervin Lang. Ervin was nearly twenty years her junior, and originally, she had pity for Ervin, as he had just lost his beautiful wife, her daughter. Blanche soon developed affections for Ervin—affections Ervin himself may not have reciprocated.

Author's rendering of Eng King. *Harrison Fillmore.*

* Monica Eng, "What's the History of Chinese Gangs in Chicago?" *Curious City* podcast, WBEZ, May 5, 2018.
† Ibid.

When Ervin later sought the attention of other women—specifically, a young woman named Josephine McKinley—Blanche became incensed.

Blanche enlisted the help of a trusted friend, Evelyn Smith. Evelyn was described as a beautiful, blonde ex-burlesque dancer with a criminal record. Evelyn was also frequently in the company of a Chinese man named Harry Jung. Blanch agreed to pay Evelyn $500, with $100 of it paid up front. Blanche received permission from Ervin to borrow $100 from him, lying that it would be used for a down payment on new furniture. Ervin approved the $100 withdrawal, and Blanche brought his own brother, William, to the bank to secure the withdrawal.

On a warm summer evening, on the second floor of 731 West Barry, the still depressed widower, Ervin, was plied with alcohol and ether until he passed out. His mother-in-law then summoned Evelyn Smith and Harry Jung. Ervin was strangled to death and his body hacked to pieces. His torso was wrapped in a blanket, and his legs were placed in a trunk Evelyn had recently purchased from the Salvation Army.

At three-thirty in the morning, Harry Jung borrowed the car of a friend named Willie Quan, the owner of a laundry at 5149 South Halsted Street. He and Evelyn loaded the mutilated body into the car and drove to Hammond, Indiana, where they threw Ervin's torso in a swamp. They hid his legs some distance away in the stump of a tree.

Blanche was hospitalized with tonsillitis the day after Ervin's torso was found in the Indiana swamp. A nurse overheard Blanche speaking to

Top: Author's rendering of Blanche Dunkel. *Harrison Fillmore.*

Bottom: Author's rendering of Evelyn Smith. *Harrison Fillmore.*

a visitor, later identified as Evelyn, who brought the day's newspaper and asked Blanche if she'd read the news. As Blanche read the headlines regarding Ervin's disappearance, Evelyn stated that she and Harry were going to New York until "this thing blows over."*

Blanche also made incriminating remarks to a relative of hers who also happened to be a Chicago police officer, telling him flatly that she had "Erv bumped off."† She was quickly taken into custody, where she made a confession naming Evelyn and Harry. Chicago police found bloody clothing at Harry Jung's laundry at 3251 West Armitage. The police, suspecting a larger involvement of the Chinese community, began rounding up Harry Jung's associates and acquaintances.

William Quan was eager to assist, according to police, and while he was suspicious of Evelyn and Harry taking his vehicle, he did not know anything about the murder. Frank and George Jung, who were both present when the police recovered the bloody clothing from Harry's laundry, both corroborated Blanche's timeline of events while adding substantial circumstantial evidence to the case. Police questioned Henry and May Moy of 226 West Alexander after receiving a tip that Evelyn and Harry had been hiding out there. After rounding up half a dozen or so other witnesses, Lieutenant William Bowler of the Chicago Police Department was quoted as saying, "We know that Jung is not a member of the On Leong or Hip Sing Tongs and as a result it would be difficult [to] hide anywhere in the proximity of Chinatown without being detected."‡

A month later, Evelyn Smith was located and arrested in New York City and extradited back to Chicago. After she also confessed, both she and Blanche were charged with Ervin Lane's murder. However, leaving Harry Jung out of the events—as Evelyn only placed him on scene as an observer—did not sit right with the Chicago Police Department's chief of detectives, John L. Sullivan, who remarked scornfully that he did not believe that "the Smith woman, slim and not too strong, carried out the work of amputation alone."§

* "Police Seek Clews to Suspects' Hideouts," *Chicago Tribune*, July 18, 1935.
† Ibid.
‡ Ibid.
§ Ibid.

Blanche Dunkel and Evelyn Smith were both found guilty of Ervin Lane's murder. Judge Cornelius Harrington sentenced the two to Dwight Women's Correctional for 180 years of hard labor. He added a special punishment to their sentence, demanding that every year, on the anniversary of the murder, both women were to spend the day in solitary confinement. Judge Harrington called it a "deterrent to crime and an admonition to criminals that you are suffering a living death." A *Chicago Tribune* article in the 1940s quoted prison officials assuring the public that the women didn't seem to mind the yearly solitary confinement: "It's a good rest for them."*

* "Two Women to Spend 14th Anniversary of Murder in Solitary," *Chicago Tribune*, July 4, 1949.

was held in custody for a little over a year before his case was dropped for lack of evidence.[129]

George Moy was facilitating the sale of a laundry business in "old" Chinatown—perhaps better described as a hostile takeover of a Hip Sing business by the On Leong Tong. Late in the afternoon, Moy was surrounded by three Hip Sing Tong members near the corner of Twenty-Second Street and Federal. During the confrontation, James Chin drew a revolver and shot Moy dead. Chin was released from custody after no witnesses would cooperate.[130]

Back in Ohio, Jack Chin Lem was applying for an appeal to his conviction. Rumors of prosecutorial misconduct and a broader On Leong conspiracy began to develop. Prosecutor Stanton wrote to the Ohio state board of clemency citing his belief that Lem may have been framed by "possible trickery by enemies of the convicts" and that the On Leong witnesses may have been lying the whole time.[131]

Jack Chin Lem's accomplices had been released after serving only three years. Jack Chin Lem himself was granted a pardon from Governor George White, with the condition that he stay out of the state of Ohio. Jack Chin Lem returned to his home in Chicago's Chinatown.

On a rainy November evening in 1937, as Jack Chin Lem walked through the streets of Chinatown, an unknown assassin ran up to him in front of his house. The assassin drew a pistol and executed him at close range. The

Chicago Tribune, reporting on the murder the next day, quoted police sources who confirmed that Jack Chin Lem remained a powerful underworld figure until his death. "Chinese ducked into their shops and homes when [Chin] came down the street, so great was their fear of him."[132] It wouldn't be the last murder in Chinatown, but the tong wars subsided considerably. The end of Prohibition and the lawlessness of the Roaring Twenties added to the security of Chinatown's safety.

In October 1937, Chinatown's organized crime lost another influential player after unofficial mayor and feared gangster Frank Moy passed away. His funeral was held at the Christian Union Church on Twenty-Third and Wentworth. His closest living relative, a distant cousin named Gerald Moy, would assume the role of Chinatown's next mayor. In what had now become typical for a man of Frank's stature, his funeral was a grandiose event complete with carriages, flying banners and a full marching band.[133]

In 1938, the Hip Sing Tong took a major blow on a national level. This time, the blow came not from problems with their rival, the On Leong, but from the federal government. United States federal narcotics agents wrapped up a long-term investigation into opium smuggling, netting a total of thirty-six leaders, nationwide, of the Hip Sing Tong. Chicago Hip Sing president Ng Yee Song was arrested in an early morning raid, along with his right-hand man, Don Bling. The investigation had been expansive: dozens of raids were executed simultaneously in Chicago, Pittsburgh, San Francisco, New York City and even Butte, Montana. Agents George H. White and John Esch, both with Chinese backgrounds, had gone deep undercover, posing as buyers. They were so convincing that they were even invited to join Chicago's Hip Sing faction.

The agents were initiated into the tong at the Chicago faction's headquarters at 422 South Clark Street. The initiates were required to change fifty dollars into silver and bring the coins to the ceremony. The agent described the ceremony as somber, with the elders dressed in traditional robes. The initiates bowed when told to do so. The coins were passed out to the elders, and whatever remained went to the president himself. The candidates then all swore an oath: "I swear to maim, rob, steal, kill or carry out any other act ordered by my superior. I will keep the secrets of the Hip Sings and accept the punishment of death if I violate my sacred oath."[134]

After infiltrating the inner sanctum of the Hip Sing, agents collected evidence exposing nationwide, Chinese-controlled opium and heroin trafficking spanning at least the last fifteen years. The Chicago president

Author's rendering of May Wong. *Harrison Fillmore.*

In the early hours of a Monday morning on the tenth of January 1939, Maria Tan Sunji was awakened by the sound of the postman ringing the bell of her apartment at 1443 West Sixty-Third Street. Maria was a student at the University of Chicago and was living with Mrs. May Wong, who was part owner of the Beverly Maid Tea restaurant at 1712 West Ninety-Fifth Street. Maria rose around eight in the morning and found May Wong in her bed with bloody sheets, unclad and beaten to death. Maria ran out of the apartment to a neighborhood grocery, where she called the police.

Detectives investigating the case learned that Maria's brother Teodoro Tan Sunji, also a student, had left the city some weeks ago and was hiding in California. Detectives intercepted letters from Teodoro asking Maria if the "Tong" was still after him. Digging further, they learned that Teodoro had plans to open up two Chinese restaurants, one at Sixty-Third and Kedzie and the other at Fifty-Ninth and Kedzie. Because of these plans, Teodoro was summoned by the On Leong Tong. It seemed they objected to Teodoro's plans. Fearing the tong, Teodoro took $800 from a safe in his apartment and fled to California.

Herbert Tsai was the other owner of the Beverly Maid Tea Restaurant. Tsai had recently completed a stint at Leavenworth for counterfeiting, having served only three years and change of a five-year penalty. Police intercepted a letter addressed to Mrs. Wong before she died from Theodoro, writing from Oakland. In the letter, Theodoro warned Mrs. Wong that "Herbert knows more than he's telling."*

On Leong executive secretary Hone Wu, second in command only to Gerald Moy, made a statement that neither Mrs. May Wong nor any employees of her restaurant had any association with or membership to the On Leong Association. He added that he did not

* "Hunt Tong Clew in Slaying of Chinese Woman," *Chicago Tribune*, January 10, 1939.

believe them to be associated with the rival Hip Sing, either.

Maria was taken to a local hotel for her protection, where she was closely guarded by a Chicago Police Department matron. During additional questioning, Maria recalled that a new employee named Arthur Hue had recently been seen in the company of Mrs. May Wong. Maria related that Hue had only been employed for approximately two weeks. Hue had recently been fired from his old employer because he had stolen twenty-eight dollars.

Author's rendering of Art Hue. *Harrison Fillmore.*

Two days later, Chicago police found Arthur Hue at 1429 North Clark Street and placed him in custody at the Englewood Police Station. Under the questioning of Captain Walter Healy and state's attorney prosecutor Julius Sherwin, Hue confessed to the murder. He stated that he arrived at Mrs. May Wong's apartment intending to get paid for prior work. After a disagreement over wages owed, he beat Mrs. Wong into submission with his shoe and then strangled her to death. He stole a total of eighteen dollars from her purse, which he spent on liquor later that evening. Captain Walter Healy acknowledged that original theories involving tong involvement were proven false.*

* "Robber Shows How He Killed Woman," *Chicago Tribune*, January 13, 1939.

of the Hip Sing, Ng Yee Song, and his right-hand man, Don Bling, would both be sentenced to nine years at Leavenworth prison. The Hip Sing Tong was in shambles nationwide. In Chicago, the organization would never fully recover, and the On Leong would further establish itself as the most powerful organization in Chinatown. The convictions only strengthened its power.

In 1938, the On Leong invented an unusual way to murder a gambler who owed a large amount of money due to mahjong losses. Edward Lo confessed to working with Barry Moy in an attempt to kill George Young, a degenerate gambler and an unemployed waiter. The two would-be assassins lured Young to dinner, and while one kept him distracted, the other planted a homemade bomb attached to an electrical light in Young's apartment. When Young returned to the apartment, he pulled the light chain, causing the bomb to explode, severely burning Young, who also suffered projectile wounds and lacerations.[135] Young would survive the attempt, but the unusual act entrenched fear in gamblers in debt to the On Leong.

CHAPTER 8

LEGITIMACY

身正不怕影子斜

"ONE WHO STANDS STRAIGHT
DOESN'T FEAR A CROOKED SHADOW"

Gerald H. Moy was born on American soil. He was a veteran of the armed forces, having served during World War I. Gerald would be responsible for the public relations shift between the citizens of Chicago and their unofficial mayor of Chinatown. Gerald Moy made certain the people knew he and his fellow Chinese citizens were fiercely patriotic Americans. He led marches demonstrating against Japan's invasion of mainland China, years before the attack at Pearl Harbor. During the war, Gerald stepped up his wartime efforts of recycling and material drives in his community.

Gerald distanced himself from organized crime, and the press covered him favorably. He was often described as neatly dressed, and reporters referenced his law degree often. When the *Chicago Tribune* reported that he had been voted in to succeed the late Frank Moy as president of the On Leong, with Hone Wu as his secretary, they referred to the On Leong as an association, rather than a tong.[136]

The assistant secretary spot had been held by Hone Wu since the late 1920s. In 1931, he was arrested and charged with attempting to bribe federal narcotics agents. Wu was convicted and sentenced to a little over two years, to be served in Leavenworth prison. Hone Wu returned to Chicago's Chinatown, keeping a low profile until he was voted in with Gerald Moy.[137]

Author's rendering of Gerald Moy. *Harrison Fillmore.*

Hone Wu was quick to give statements to newspapers to distance the On Leong from any trouble. He denied any recent tong violence, and if a murder should occur, such as Mrs. May Wong's murder, he was quick to deny an organized criminal motive.[138] Hone Wu, who had also registered for the draft during World War I, became involved with the World War II charity Chinese Relief Fund Association.

In 1942, Hone Wu took on the position of commander in the Office of Civilian Defense war effort. During a parade in downtown Chicago to show solidarity with the United Nations, Hone Wu brought more than 1,500 Chinatown residents to the march. Hone Wu would remain the mysterious, more traditional face of the On Leong Tong, even as Gerald H. Moy made steps to legitimize the organization.

Author's rendering of Harry Lee. *Harrison Fillmore.*

Shortly after becoming the unofficial mayor of Chinatown, Gerald married Alice Gee Kee. They were married in a "secret" Chinese ceremony before the lavish service that was held at the Christian Chinese Congregational Union Church. Newspapers commented on the "American looking" bridegroom in a "dark business suit with a white carnation on his lapel."[139] The reception was held at the Tin Yen restaurant at 2257 South Wentworth. It was reported that every guest was required to bring a gift of at least ten dollars for the bride and groom.[140]

One of the On Leong's ranking secretaries made the news in 1946. Harry Lee, who called himself a retired cafe owner, was the victim of a violent home invasion. Two offenders broke into Harry Lee's apartment and then tied up him and his wife, hand and foot, while the men ransacked the premises. The offenders found $2,000 in cash and what was estimated at over $2,000 worth of jewelry. As the robbers finished their score, Harry Lee began to wriggle out of the rope. The robbers escaped the apartment, running down the stairs just as Harry Lee freed himself. The men attempted to flee from the building, but not before Harry Lee retrieved a gun and shot at the culprits three times from his apartment window.

Ex-convict Tony Palsastro, aka Fred A. Lucas, who had recently been paroled for robbery, was struck and killed. Palsastro fell to the street, dropping one of Harry Lee's wife's rings; however, the second man escaped with most of the proceeds. Chicago police cleared Harry Hee of any wrongdoing.[141]

Gerald Moy's rule as mayor of Chinatown wasn't completely without scandal. In 1950, Frank Lung, a prominent member of the community and owner of the popular Phoenix Inn Chinese restaurant in Evanston, went missing. Investigators learned that Lung was a high-stakes gambler and that his game of choice was Fan Tan. He was on a losing streak and owed money all over Chinatown.[142] Frank Lung's family members were desperate, pleading for the public's help. The fear of foul play and the old On Leong ways loomed over the missing man's fate. There was also suspicion that a man that far in debt would have motive to disappear. Two weeks later, Frank Lung's body washed up on the shore of Lake Michigan near Ninety-Ninth Street. A motive was never determined.

The Ling Long Museum in the heart of Chinatown was built in an effort to boost tourism and promote relations. Gerald Moy was the catalyst behind creating the museum and continued to foster goodwill with the rest of the city. The museum distributed a publication printed by the local *San Min Morning Paper*, and within, Gerald included a detailed description of the once secret and mysterious tongs. Looking to set the record straight for any curious visitor, the tourist publication explained:

> *There is really no political set-up in Chinatown. We have no "mayor" or "cityhall." Chinatown is, on the other hand, self-governed by Chinese without political alliances through the cooperation of the different alliances. What is commonly called the "city hall" is the On Leong Merchants Association Building. The so-called "mayor"' is in reality one of the secretaries of the Association....*
>
> *The so frequently mentioned "tongs" are simply merchant associations and strictly of American origin. The purposes of all tongs are beneficial and protective, but sometimes misdemeanors committed by individual members are unjustly ascribed to the tong and gain it unfavorable repute.*

The Chinese Christian Church. *Photograph by author.*

> *Tong leaders today are far more progressive than in the past and oftentimes well educated men from Chinese and American Universities. Their efforts are directed towards philanthropic work rather than confined to rivalry. It has been at least five years since any serious dispute or trouble.*[143]

Gerald Moy continued his fundraising and philanthropy. In 1947, he raised over $1,000 for the construction of a new church for the Chinese Christian Union at 2301 South Wentworth. In 1950, he was quoted in the *Chicago Tribune* after Cold War tensions rose between the United States and China. In the article, Gerald Moy asserted that the Chinese in Chicago were loyal to the United States and would remain so, even if it was at war with communist China. In an age of heightened suspicion and anti-communist hearings, Gerald Moy stated, "We don't like those Reds."[144]

In the summer of 1956, Gerald H. Moy passed away from natural causes. His funeral was held at the same Chinese Christian Union Church that he helped build. Behind the hearse marched hundreds of friends and family members accompanied by an American Legion military marching band.

During Gerald Moy's tenure as mayor of Chinatown, a vicious gang of half-Chinese brothers rained terror on Chinese businesses. The Wings—William, Arthur and George—began robbing laundries all over Chicago. During a robbery at 643 North Cicero, they stabbed to death an employee named King Lee. They also murdered the owner of another laundry during a robbery. Sam Wing was beaten to death by the brothers in his laundry at 34 East 115th Street. Police eventually caught up with the brothers and ended their crime spree. After the arrests, William Wing gave a statement to detectives that they, the brothers, "hated all Chinese."*

* "Police to Quiz 3 Brothers in Chinese Deaths," *Chicago Tribune*, January 22, 1947.

The former mayor of Chinatown, and the head of the On Leong Merchants Association, as it was now known, was largely responsible for changing the public's perception of the Chinatown organization, no longer viewed as a criminal organization and rarely referred to any longer as a tong. Gerald Moy successfully rebranded the On Leong into a benevolent association founded for the purposes of aid and assistance.

Gerald Moy's successor was to be his cousin Wilson W. Moy, a man who would erase all the hard work Gerald Moy put in to legitimize the On Leong and change public perception of the tong.

Wilson Moy would apply some of the lessons learned from Gerald's advocacy and diplomacy. He was active in the Red Cross and made many statements mirroring Gerald's dislike for communists and for the government of China.[145] He was outspokenly patriotic to the United States and was active in many charities and political committees. What Wilson Moy also did was ramp up the gambling interests in Chinatown. The On Leong also took a stronger stance under Wilson, essentially demanding membership from every business owner and collecting dues. The rackets were also heavily taxed. Anyone in Chinatown who made a profit gleaned from an illegal enterprise owed a percentage to the On Leong Association. That included prostitution, narcotics, human trafficking and, of course, gambling.

Harry P. Lee also became vocal in his opposition to the communists. Harry, whose claim to fame was shooting and killing one of the men who broke into

Author's rendering of Wilson Moy. *Harrison Fillmore.*

his home, was voted in as Wilson H. Moy's secretary, essentially making him number two in the On Leong. After the Associated Press ran a story about Chinese communists threatening American Chinese family members in order to extort money, Harry P. Lee dismissed the notion. Harry explained to *Chicago Tribune* reporters that it would be "foolish" to pay any blackmail money and that the scheme would never work against the Chinese people in the States.[146]

With very little to worry about from the rival Hip Sings and with the police department's seemingly lax enforcement in general, gambling in Chinatown became more open and notorious. Chicago Police from the Deering station broke up a large, high-stakes mahjong game at the Chinese American Legion Post. After Cook County judge Oscar Caplan threw out the case, the arrestees organized and filed a lawsuit against Lieutenant McLaughlin, who was in charge of the raid, and his officers, claiming the gamblers were falsely arrested.[147] If the On Leong's intention in suing members of the Chicago Police Department was to deter further police enforcement action, it was not successful. Several raids followed, and heavy-handed enforcement continued well into the late 1960s.

The underground casinos in Chinatown often changed locations in an effort to avoid detection. A successful raid on an abandoned storefront at 209 West Cermak was tempered by the fact that the proprietors of the joint had been arrested only two weeks prior while running games in a building at 214 West Twenty-Second Place. The casino had merely moved across the back alley.

Other than the occasional gambling den raid and a few rare arrests for prostitution, the 1950s and '60s were a relatively quiet time for Chinatown. During the same time, the Chinese population in Chicago nearly doubled. The On Leong Merchants Association and the Hip Sings both played an important role as institutions assisting the new immigrants.

In the early 1970s, the president of the Hip Sings, Jimmy Wong, officially announced the move to "New" Chinatown centered on Argyle Street and Broadway.[148] The tiny enclave in Uptown had been attracting Asian immigrants for more than a decade, and the recent population growth added

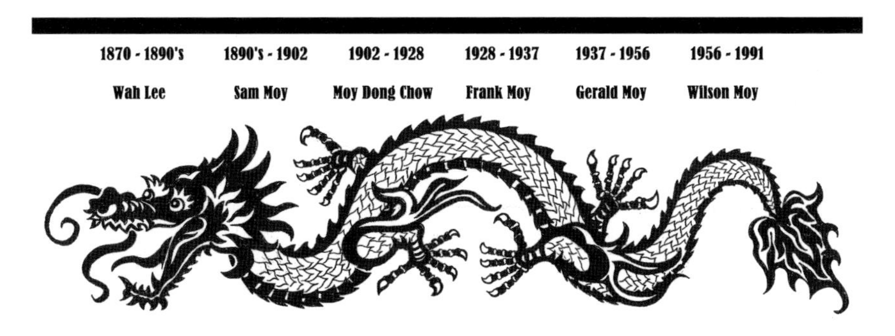

Author's rendering of Godfathers of Chinatown timeline. *Harrison Fillmore.*

to their strength in numbers. Jimmy Wong and his Hip Sing brought together a group of investors and claimed nearly half of the local real estate along Argyle Street. Aside from building the new Hip Sing headquarters, they also supported new restaurants, stores and gift shops in the area. They even hired local architect T.C. Chang for a conceptual vision of how the neighborhood should look. The industrious move wasn't completely voluntary. The federal government had claimed eminent domain, paying $300,000 for the last few dilapidated structures and flophouses left in the "Old" Chinatown at Van Buren and Clark Streets. The old Hip Sing headquarters was razed to make way for a new federal corrections facility and its neighboring parking lot.

The lines were now clearly drawn, the territories claimed. The Hip Sings would now control interests in the New Chinatown, sometimes called Little Chinatown, while the On Leong Merchants Association would retain its dominance in place.

CHAPTER 9

HONG CHING: THE NEW ONES

千军易得, 一将难求

"It's Easy to Find a Thousand Soldiers, but a Good General Is Hard to Find"

With the sudden rise in Chinese immigrants came new youth gangs. Many began as loosely affiliated cliques. Some were formed to provide protection from the nearby Harold Ickes housing projects, located just east of the expressway. Others were formed for nothing more than mischief and petty crimes.

In the late sixties, the Juk Sing gang, also known as ABC—which stood for "American-born Chinese"—began as a rivalry to the FOBs. The FOBs, or "Fresh on Board," was a youth gang composed of new immigrants and sometimes referred to as Juk Tuk, meaning "born in China." Finding themselves as new residents in Chicago's Chinatown, these immigrants formed a gang for the purpose of their own protection. New immigrants were often victims of aggression and extortion by the older and more established organized criminal element. The FOBs sought to fight that head-on. Neither gang lasted more than a few years, as more organized gangs became prominent, mirroring the youth gang trends that changed the organized criminal element in the city. Other short-lived youth gangs included the Flying Dragons, who remained prominent in New York City, and the Wah Chings from California. Neither gang lasted very long in Chicago's Chinatown.

The Chinese Freemasons was a loosely associated fraternal group dating to the beginning of the twentieth century. It existed for social activities, for the most part, and headed several clubhouses over the years. The Chicago Police Department Intelligence Section identified a group of Chinese youths calling themselves the Freemasons and officially documented them as a "gang" in 1990. The youth gang had very little, if any, association with the original Freemasons. Members frequented the China City Lounge at Cermak and Clark and the Freemason clubhouse at 211 West Cermak. Despite a few street fights and attempts to recruit new, young members, the street gang dissolved after only a few years. The original Chinese Freemasons lodge continued to thrive with no criminal activity ever attributed to their official organization.[149]

The White Eagles and the Black Eagles gained notoriety in the city's second New Chinatown on the north side, not to be confused or associated with the White or Black Eagles from New York City. The White Eagles never grew large enough to claim any real territory as they were primarily younger members, waiting their turn to become Black Eagles. The gang dissipated as members grew older and turned into fully sworn members of the Black Eagles. With the influx of lower East Asian immigrants, the Black Eagles had members of Vietnamese, Cambodian and Laotian descent mixed in with its Chinese members. Chicago police connected the Black Eagles to a series of home invasions and small store robberies in the eighties. All the gang's victims were of Asian descent, supporting the department's theory that the gangs only victimize their own people.

Chicago's New Chinatown on the north side was also the breeding ground for the Da Nang gang, composed of strictly Vietnamese members, and the Vuong Cao, which took in members from several different backgrounds but was majority Vietnamese. Interestingly, both gangs were loyal underlings to the Hip Sing, which had established dominance in Chicago's New Chinatown and were seen as the overall leaders of all organized crime within. Da Nang gang members were neighborhood street fighters and quick with weapons in a street fight. The Vuong Cao became known for car theft rings. The gang became involved in retagging stolen vehicles with fictitious VINs and exporting stolen parts and whole vehicles to Asia. The Vuong Cao became the first known organized group to use "jiggle keys" to steal vehicles.[150] One GM model vehicle's ignition keys would fit one in approximately twenty like vehicles. Someone with a lot of time on their hands could walk the city searching for similar models and testing their keys until they found a match. Japanese models were closer to

Above: Looking eastbound on Argyle Street, "New" Chinatown. *Photograph by author.*

Left: The Hip Sing headquarters. *Photograph by author.*

one in seven. The thieves learned that by filing down keys, smoothing them over on their teeth to fit more models, they simply had to jiggle the keys in the ignition until the tumblers fell into place and the ignition could be turned. They were known to use electrical tape on their fingertips to avoid leaving evidence and because ripping them off after a police stop was less conspicuous than wearing gloves. Vuong Cao gang members came to be known by police for their taste in fancy, expensive sports cars.

Flip City began as a loose affiliated "party crew." In the late seventies and early eighties, these crews, which developed much like other small factions in the city, grew in numbers and then in criminal activity. Flip City, while Asian at its core, included Filipino, Korean and Chinese members but had no strict ethnic policy and accepted recruits from all backgrounds. As Flip City members became involved with street fights and larger rivalries, they became more of a street gang and affiliated themselves with the more established, national Latin King street gang. Leader King Droopy soon changed the gang's name to the Flip City Crowns. Several offshoot factions were also created, including the Flip City Brotherhood and Flip Paradise. The gang changed again to Flip City Kings to further show its allegiance to the Latin Kings. In the early nineties, the Latin King Nation as a whole decided to eliminate all associates, demanding groups like the Assyrian Kings, the Milwaukee Kings and the Flip City Kings drop their original names and become Latin Kings outright. Refusal to do so meant they were instant enemies. With the incarceration of their de facto leader, King Droopy, for a federal ecstasy distribution arrest, and after meeting the Latin King Nation's demands, Flip City ceased to exist. A faction of former Flip City members survived as Akhros—which was a Manila university fraternity reference, from the Alpha Kappa Rhos—but they became more of an old school "party crew" than an actual street gang.

Cambodian youths who were new immigrants began the Loco Boyz gang in uptown Chicago. Its numbers were never particularly strong, and the gang weakened further after members broke off to align themselves with the California Bloods. The split factions became the OLBs, or Original Loco Boyz, and the Outlaw Loco Bloods and mainly fought each other. A wave of deportations for criminal convictions effectively diminished their ranks in the 1990s until both gangs dissipated.

The Scorpions was another street gang that didn't last past a single generation of teen members. The gang was also from the Uptown neighborhood and, while predominantly Vietnamese, it had Filipino and Hispanic members, as well. The gang died out before the larger consolidation of People versus Folks alignment created in the Illinois prison system in the late eighties and early nineties.

Youth gangs were often breeding grounds for organized criminal groups like the On Leong. They were similar to minor league teams, with the larger, stronger criminal organizations plucking particularly useful members into their organizations. The On Leong had its own "youth group" called the Quon Ying, better known as the Ghost Shadows. Much like how the history of the origination of the tongs is mired in fact and legend, so too the story of the Ghost Shadow moniker. In New York City, a band of unnamed youths wreaking havoc on the streets of Chinatown was known as troublemakers but not yet as established, hardened criminals. They were known to frequent local restaurants and then refuse to pay the bill. While at first, they simply ran away, ditching the bill, as they grew bolder, they would sign the bill with the Chinese characters for "Ghost Shadows" and walk out on the bill. Local authorities investigating the youth group began calling them by the Chinese characters they used to sign the bills, and the group later adopted the name. A Chicago newspaper even referenced the same story in 1981. Instead of paying their restaurant bill in the heart of Chinatown, four "hard-looking Orientals"[151] scrawled the words "Ghost Shadows" on the bill and left the place. Another legend comes from the *New York Times*, which claimed that while interviewing a member of the White Eagles street gang, its reporter asked what the rival Quon Ying gang's name meant. The reporter deduced that the name translated to "not an eagle," but the gang member stated that "Ghost Shadow" was meant to be an insult. The gangs had long called white people Hak Guey, meaning "white ghost," as a derogatory term. To label someone a ghost meant they weren't whole; they weren't a person. To name them a ghost and a shadow was a double insult.[152]

The Ghost Shadows began in New York City as a group of street toughs. The larger On Leong soon found them useful for more than just gang fights and petty larceny. In 1974, the Ghost Shadows were officially recognized by the On Leong Tong and sanctioned as an affiliate membership. In simple terms, this meant paying dues to the On Leong, as well as handing over a percentage of any funds obtained illegally. The On Leong adopted the gang as its enforcement arm, providing protection for its gambling clubs. As trust grew and as the new affiliate proved its efficiency, the On Leong began to use the Ghost Shadows for everything from extortion to murder. The Ghost Shadow gang soon opened a faction in Chicago, among

Author's rendering of Ghost Shadow Chinese characters. *Harrison Fillmore.*

other cities across the nation. The Ghost Shadows had twenty-five original members when it began in Chicago.

Members of the Ghost Shadows were prohibited from extorting store owners and restaurateurs who were already paying protection to the On Leong. For collecting these dues, they were paid a percentage, but unapproved extortion was a violation, although it did occur occasionally. But because of the strict policy, Ghost Shadow members often deferred to committing street robberies and burglaries. If the victim was later found to be protected by the On Leong, a compromise was worked out. Sometimes, the gang paid a fee to the On Leong for the compensation of the victimized party. Most of that money was kept by the On Leong itself, with very little making its way back to the victim. If the victim was a member of the On Leong in good standing, more expensive fines were levied and with them, an official verbal, in-person apology was required. The commonality with all these crimes was that the Chicago Police Department was not to be involved. The On Leong policed the community.

The Ghost Shadows evolved from being a youth gang to becoming its own criminal enterprise. It followed a strict hierarchy. The Dai Lo was the ultimate leader of the gang. Older members could be called Dai Lo, as it was translated to mean "Big Brother," but there was only one main Dai Lo. Next in the pecking order were the Ghost Shadow gang lieutenants. Normally, they had a crew of ten or so members under them to direct, counsel and guide. The soldiers of the Ghost Shadows were called Mah-Jai, or "little horses." They were the street toughs on whom the Ghost Shadows depended. For a time, the Ghost Shadows in Chicago had a younger gang faction of their own. The Gray Ghosts held some prominence for a time as underlings to the Ghost Shadows. They were members in training, serving a probationary period before being allowed to join the Ghost Shadows. The young organization quickly died out in the mid- to late eighties, with many of its members either moving away, going legitimate or joining the ranks of the Ghost Shadows. After the Gray Ghosts dissolved, the young members, waiting to be officially sworn in as gang members, were simply named the Hong Chings, or the "New Ones."

While still loyal to the On Leong, the Ghost Shadows took on new illegal operations, including intricate car theft rings, narcotics trafficking, human trafficking and their own brand and victims of extortion. Their modus operandi quickly became recognizable. A group of five members or so would enter an unaffiliated Asian-owned business, often a restaurant or laundry, and request to speak to the owner. One of the gang would then request money from the owner under the guise of building a youth clubhouse. Occasionally, they would request the money as part of a collection to bail out a brother Chinese member, possibly wronged while defending Chinatown's interests. Resistance was met with subtle threats. One member might open his jacket to show he was armed. Another might imply repercussions for noncooperation. If the owner resisted handing over cash outright, the Ghost Shadows used washed checks they knew to be worthless, giving the owner or manager a paper trail with which he could claim plausible deniability. The Ghost Shadows were well trained by the On Leong, which demanded that violence only be used in extreme situations. The gang members, it seemed, were well disciplined. That all changed in the spring of 1977.

CHAPTER 10

THE HIP SING ROBBERY

芒刺在背

"A Thorn in One's Flesh"

It was the end of the Chinese New Year season. Jimmy Wong, president of the Hip Sings, was hosting a party on the second floor of the gang's new clubhouse at 1123 West Argyle Street. Approximately 150 people attended the party; many were members and associates of the Hip Sings, but there were plenty of unaffiliated gamblers in attendance, as well. Hip Sing secretary Joseph Leung was working security at the front of the establishment when a Chinese man he had never seen before came to the entrance door. Leung found it odd that the man entered the party only momentarily and quickly departed. However, Leung was not alarmed, as the party was an "open house" and there were several Chinese men whom he did not recognize. Prior to that incident, none of the Hip Sing gambling dens had been robbed since the move north, and the rivalry with the On Leong had been dormant for a long time.

At one thirty in the morning, the man returned. Behind him were seven members of the Ghost Shadows, two of them wearing ski masks as they barged into the banquet room. They were all armed with matching .38-caliber blue steel revolvers and spoke in a heavy Cantonese accent as they announced the robbery.

5220 North Sheridan Avenue. *Photograph by author.*

The announcement caused momentary chaos as gamblers scrambled to their feet and attempted to hide money. One of the Ghost Shadows, wearing a black trench coat, struck an eighty-year-old man in the face with his pistol. The old man fell to the floor, bleeding. The violent entrance successfully controlled the rest of the victims, who complied with the robbers' demands.

The victims were ordered to lie on the floor and place all their valuables in front of them. The offenders wanted cash, wallets, watches and jewelry. As two Ghost Shadow members worked the floor, collecting the loot, the victims were forced to remove their trousers, ostensibly to buy the Ghost Shadows time for their getaway. The Ghost Shadow members began to argue among themselves. In Cantonese, they bickered about recovering all the valuables in the room.

One of the Ghost Shadows caught a victim attempting to hide his watch by pushing it up his sleeve. The Ghost Shadow member pistol-whipped the man's head and face. None of the victims attempted to hide anything of value after that.

At one point, two of the offenders demanded that the men remove their undergarments to ensure no one had hidden anything of value. After they were satisfied, having recovered everything of value from every victim, they ordered the victims at gunpoint to stand against the west end of the room and face the wall. The victims were told to wait fifteen minutes before leaving the wall and were warned not to call the police. The Ghost Shadows made their escape.

Jimmy Wong personally lost over $500. The bandits had also taken his jade ring set in pure gold and a $2,000 watch. The Hip Sing president told responding detectives that no gambling had occurred prior to the robbery, contradicting every other victim that evening. He later admitted that customers may have been playing a card game or two.[153]

Joseph Leung, the Hip Sings' secretary, number two in the organization, was much more forthright. Leung cooperated with detectives and explained how he suspected the men in ski masks to be local Ghost Shadow members whom he would normally recognize, hence the disguise. He also related that he suspected some of these offenders to be the men who robbed a gambling den a month before, but the details of that robbery remained unreported and sketchy. Leung explained that the On Leong controlled Chicago's Chinatown at Cermak and Wentworth and that the Hip Sings ran the smaller, newer Chinatown on Argyle Street. He admitted that they were still rivals but were not at war like they had been in the 1920s. Most disagreements were handled in a diplomatic manner; however, he blamed the On Leong for allowing this younger gang to victimize Hip Sing–associated targets.[154]

The brazen robbery made the newspapers, and Asian organized crime was back in the headlines, something that hadn't happened with any regularity since the tong wars in the 1920s. Suddenly, there was a new effort to investigate and prosecute Chinatown's criminal organizations. Mayor Daley made a public statement that unlike New York and San Francisco, the city of Chicago had never had an Asian crime problem.[155] He followed that up with the appointment of a special prosecutor specifically designated to prosecute any criminal investigations.

Wilson Moy, the recognized mayor of Chinatown, disavowed any relationship between the Ghost Shadows and the On Leong Association, of which he remained president. Speaking to reporters regarding the robbery, Wilson Moy said of the Ghost Shadows, "These are drifters. They think that we owe them something and that they should have been in this country a long time ago, but because of the immigration quotas, they couldn't get in until now. They feel they have to take it out on somebody." Wilson continued to downplay the event and any connection to a larger conspiracy. "The last killing we had here must have been 1929. When I was a kid they used to talk about the killings between the Tongs, but there were so few even back then it didn't amount to anything."[156]

Despite Wilson Moy's insistence that this was an isolated incident, the Chicago Police Department ramped up its efforts to investigate Asian organized crime. The Intelligence Unit dedicated several officers to the efforts and assigned several gang specialists. While giving special attention to the new tensions, tactical officers observed a man acting suspiciously in the heart of Chinatown. It appeared that he was holding a long gun, and when they approached, they learned that he was armed with a .22-caliber rifle, a sawed-off 12-gauge shotgun and a .357 Colt Python revolver. The man's motive was never determined, and a language barrier hampered any meaningful interrogation, but it was speculated he was either selling the weapons or arming fellow gang members against possible retaliation. A short time after that, police raided another On Leong safe house. They recovered four weapons and a large quantity of ammunition.

Police interviewed a Hip Sing member who wished to remain anonymous. He told the police that he read about the Ghost Shadows in Chinese-language newspapers and that their reputation in New York City and San Francisco caused him to fear for his life here in Chicago. The confidential informant told investigators that the Ghost Shadows did not have a club or headquarters but could be found frequenting the China Doll Club at 6312 North Broadway. The Ghost Shadows had been in Chicago for some time, but a recent transplant from New York City named Kong Ming "Raymond" Li had taken over in 1976 and was causing trouble.[157]

Detectives pushed the Hip Sing robbery case forward. They followed leads and reinterviewed witnesses. They visited many Chinese establishments in Chicago, as well as restaurants in northwest Indiana, speaking to owners, workers and recent immigrants. While building their armed robbery case, they learned of another daring home invasion robbery of a Hip Sing gun collector.

The gun collector's wife told detectives that three Chinese males came to her door and asked to speak to one of her sons. She feared retaliation of some sort, knowing that her sons were involved with street gangs, and did not immediately open the door. One of the men then forced his way through the door and grabbed the woman by her throat. Hearing the commotion, the gun collector came to the front room, where he observed the three offenders, each armed with blue steel revolvers identical to the weapons used in the Hip Sing robbery. One of the offenders pointed the weapon at the victim's head and, addressing him by his first name, announced that they "only wanted the guns."[158] Both of the victims were ordered to lie on the ground. As one of the offenders held the couple at gunpoint, the other two walked directly to the back bedroom and removed a safe. It was clear that either they had been in the apartment before or someone had told them exactly where to find the guns. The offenders wrapped the safe in a sheet and removed a decorative rifle from a wall. They tied up the couple and told the victims that if they called the police, they would return to kill them. After the three offenders exited, the wife was able to release herself from her bindings and ran to the window to see them escape in a white work van with a red stripe on the front. The stolen property included a .22-caliber rifle, a .25-caliber revolver, a .38-caliber revolver and two .32-caliber automatics. A week later, the safe was found forty miles south of the city, cracked open and empty on the side of a rural road near Manteno, Illinois.

Detectives interviewed the gun collector's sons. They were asked if there had been anyone in the apartment recently who knew about the guns. The boys came up with one name: Ming. But they insisted it couldn't have been Ming because he was a close family friend and a member of the Hip Sing. The sons thought he would never cooperate with the Ghost Shadows.

Detectives identified and kept a close eye on Ming. During an interview, Ming had given detectives an alibi for the time of the robbery and denied any involvement. Ming was later observed with members of the Ghost Shadows at the Dragon Q pool hall at 202 West Cermak. One of them drove a white work van with a red stripe. Detectives learned that the van was registered to the owner of a Chinese restaurant in Manteno, Illinois. Ming had listed his residence using the address of that same Manteno restaurant.

Detectives following leads identified three offenders, all members of the Ghost Shadows. Because of Ming's association with that group, and because they suspected that he had set up the home invasion, he was also identified as a possible suspect. Detectives met with the gun collector's wife, and she was presented with a photo lineup with all four offenders' mug shots from prior arrests. She positively identified the three Ghost Shadow gang members as well as Ming, whom she knew to have been in the home just prior to the incident.

Allen "Fat Pig" Li, Dave Chow, Wing Eng and Ming were arrested and brought to the Detective Division for a lineup. During interrogations, the offenders admitted their roles in the home invasion. They also told the detectives that they were confident they would beat the case. They did not expect an approval of charges, and if police officers insisted, they were sure they would win in court. The detectives described all four offenders, while admitting guilt, as "cocky."[159] The state's attorney's special prosecutor was on hand to approve charges in the case and to lock in any statements. The gun collector, his wife and their sons arrived together at the station, and the case quickly began to fall apart.

According to the detectives, the family began arguing among themselves. The gun collector's sons insisted that their mother had identified the wrong men. The wife changed her statement and was now unsure of her previous identification. The gun collector outright refused to prosecute. Without an identification and without cooperation, the state's attorney dismissed the charges and released all four Ghost Shadow members.

After the men were released, detectives interviewed the gun collector's eldest son one last time. He admitted that the four freed men were indeed the offenders, but he and his family feared repercussions not only from the Ghost Shadows but also from both the Hip Sing and the On Leong Tongs. He admitted to being a member of the Hip Sings, and detectives further determined that he was present the night of the Hip Sing gambling den robbery.

The gun collector's son made one final and chilling statement to the detectives. He stated that he would never forget what the offenders had done to him and that he did not want any law enforcement help in these matters. He told detectives that he would deal with it the "Chinese way."[160]

As law enforcement stepped up its intelligence operations, Allen Li was identified as the leader of the Ghost Shadows. Police began to put more pressure on the gang. Arrests and small raids followed, but police efforts did little to curtail the rising wave of crime brought by the Ghost Shadows. Investigators knew they were involved with mass extortion schemes all across the city and Chinatown, but they could not find any victims who were willing to cooperate. As the gun collector's son stated, most would handle it the "Chinese way"—that was, until a member of the Moy family had had enough.

This mechanic ran a garage in Chinatown. He was a Moy family member and had faithfully paid his dues for years to both the Moy Family Association and the On Leong. He did not drink or gamble, and he had never gone to the On Leong for any help in the past. His business was self-made, and he took pride in his success in the United States. In the fall of 1977, the mechanic received his first visit from members of the Ghost Shadows. Five offenders entered his shop and demanded money. He was able to convince the gang members that the little money he had in the shop at the time was for his rent but that he would be willing to make a payment in one week's time. The Ghost Shadow members agreed to the delay but threatened physical harm if he did not pay at their next visit, and they warned him not to go to the police.

The mechanic did not report the incident to the police but instead went to the On Leong Association. He pleaded for the association's help with the extortionists. After all, he'd been dutifully paying for its "protection" nearly all his adult life. The On Leong, however, had problems of its own. The mechanic wasn't the only member of the Chinatown business community complaining about the new Ghost Shadows and their heavy-handed tactics. While the On Leong elders knew how to utilize the new enforcement arm of their association, they clearly could not control all of the Ghost Shadow gang's criminal proclivities.

When the Ghost Shadow members arrived the following week, the mechanic felt he had no choice and forked over one hundred dollars to the Ghost Shadows. Another week passed, and the gang members returned. The mechanic claimed business was poor and offered only sixty dollars. This angered the extortionists, who demanded more money. The Ghost Shadows swore to return and threatened physical violence if the mechanic did not pay up.

The mechanic turned to the Chicago Police Department. A tactical unit was put on the case, and an operation began to pursue the offenders. On the agreed-on date, the mechanic was given two marked fifty-dollar bills from CPD contingency funds. "Marked" meant simply that law enforcement recorded the bills' serial numbers for later recovery and identification. Heavy surveillance was placed on the mechanic's shop, with enforcement officers near and at the ready.

Randy Eng arrived at the mechanic's shop under the careful eye of law enforcement. The mechanic recognized Eng as having been one of the Ghost Shadow gang members that arrived and demanded money that very first day. The mechanic refused to pay Eng alone. Eng left the premises but soon returned with David Wong. The mechanic recognized David Wong as the Ghost Shadow gang member who had done most of the talking. It was his belief that Wong held some sort of leadership role within the Ghost Shadows. The mechanic attempted once more to avoid the payout, claiming he was behind on rent once again. Wong told the mechanic that if he refused to hand over the money, he "would no longer need rent money" because he was going to "hurt the mechanic so that he wouldn't be able to work."[161] The mechanic handed over the two fifty-dollar bills from Chicago police's prerecorded funds.

The two Ghost Shadow members left the mechanic's shop. A short distance away, the enforcement officers closed in. The two members fled on sight of the unmarked squad car, and a foot chase ensued. Both Ghost Shadow members were apprehended, and Wong was found to have the marked money in his possession.[162]

The arrests barely made a blip on the radar of Chinatown's organized crime. But this was the first operation of its kind and showed that the criminal element's grip on ordinary citizens was beginning to slip.

Kong Ming "Raymond" Ly, aka "Fan Chun" (Rice Scoop), drove a pearl white, brand-new Pontiac Firebird. He had long black hair and wore designer clothes. He hailed from Toronto, Canada, by way of New York City, and if he'd come to Chicago to keep a low profile, he wasn't doing a very good job of it. Ly was suspected of taking part in the Hip Sing robbery, if not leading it. Chicago police began to focus their investigation on Ly, sharing information with Toronto and New York City law enforcement authorities. Toronto authorities suspected Ly to be a major smuggler of both firearms and narcotics. New York City suspected him of committing a murder.[163]

While acting as the leader for the Ghost Shadows in Chicago and nationwide, Ly was also a full-fledged member of the On Leong Association. Ly owned a kung fu club in "New" Chinatown—oddly, in Hip Sing territory on Argyle Street—named the Seven Star Praying Mantis. He split his time residing in two apartments, each with a different woman. He traveled often, moving to and from cities across the United States, including Boston, New York City and Washington, D.C. He was a member of the "Ghost City," which was the unofficial name for the group of Ghost Shadow leaders from across the nation, of which he was the recognized head.

Investigators in Chicago learned that Toronto police had conducted a search warrant of Ly's premises. Recovered during the execution of that search warrant were several ledgers containing evidence of a large-scale international extortion racket. They also recovered what they believed to be Ghost Shadow membership records from Toronto and several U.S. cities. They believed that Ly had come to Chicago to avoid prosecution. New York City authorities suspected Ly was hiding out in Chicago to avoid murder charges there.

Information from other jurisdictions began to come to light. Evanston police suspected Ghost Shadow gang members to be responsible for a takeover-style armed robbery at the Phoenix Inn Chinese restaurant at 608 West Davis Street. The Chinese owner of the establishment refused to cooperate with authorities, and the only information regarding the incident came from a customer who was not of Chinese descent but was present at the time.[164] Authorities in Racine, Wisconsin, reported a similar incident and

1123 West Argyle Street. *Photograph by author.*

arrested four offenders, all members of the Ghost Shadow gang.[165] Again, none of the victims cooperated in the prosecution, and all the gang members were released without charges.

The Far East restaurant at 5220 North Sheridan was under the protection of the Hip Sings. That didn't stop twenty or so Ghost Shadow gang members from dining there, Dave Chow among them. After racking up a healthy bill, the Ghost Shadows refused to pay. The proprietor of the establishment got into a heated argument with the gang members. The confrontation became violent when the Ghost Shadows began to batter the owner and the employees. During the fracas, gang members broke dishes and glasses, flipped over tables and caused other property damage. Responding police arrested several Ghost Shadow members, including Dave Chow.[166]

The Chicago faction of the Hip Sings was losing its patience with the Ghost Shadows. The On Leong disowned the gang publicly, and the Hip Sing's requests for the larger organization to control its own fell upon deaf ears. The Hip Sings sent word to New York City; they needed soldiers.

Chicago police responded to a "man shot" in an apartment a few blocks north of New Chinatown. The victim was shot in his side but survived his injury. Investigators learned that the gunman belonged to the Hip Sing's own sub-faction of hired guns called the Taiwan Brothers.

The Taiwan Brothers was a very loosely affiliated group of soldiers who were all members of or associated with the Hip Sings. They had none of the organization the Ghost Shadows had at the time and were tied together geographically because most members were direct immigrants from Taiwan. The Hip Sings utilized the Taiwan Brothers often for security for their various rackets, but up until the recent rise of Ghost Shadow crime, they had not used the Taiwan Brothers as their enforcement arm. That changed when Hip Sing leader Jason Wang met four Hip Sing Taiwan Brothers from New York City.

Chicago police investigators developed an informant who related that he and three others were recruited in New York City by the Hip Sings. They were told that the Chicago Hip Sings needed muscle and that they were to report to Jason Wang, national leader of the Taiwan Brothers. The informant stated that the Taiwan Brothers and the Ghost Shadows were known enemies. Aside from working security for the Hip Sings, they were tasked with collecting intelligence on the Ghost Shadows and reporting back to Wang.[167]

Jason Wang was arrested for the shooting because police discovered him near the scene and recovered the weapon. The weapon had been reported as stolen out of Washington, D.C. Although he was charged, the case went nowhere as the victim recovered and refused to cooperate or testify in court.

After Dave Chow's frequent brushes with the law in Illinois and following the gun collector's arrest, he relocated to New York City. He and four other Ghost Shadow gang members committed a takeover-style armed robbery of the Jade House restaurant in Stratford, New Jersey. After barging into the place, they ordered everyone to the ground at gunpoint. They bound the restaurant employees with rope. One of the restaurant's patrons happened to be an off-duty police officer with his family. Fearing an execution-style mass shooting, the officer announced himself while drawing his weapon, which resulted in a shoot-out. When the dust settled, Ghost Shadow gang member George Chew had been fatally shot in the chest. Two innocent victims suffered minor injuries when the Ghost Shadows opened fire.[168]

David Chow was arrested, and a follow-up search warrant executed by the New York City Police Department found one of the weapons taken from the home invasion of the gun collector in Chicago, showing a true pipeline of arms across state lines by the Ghost Shadows. Also arrested were William "Horse" Tung and Dennis Chan. The getaway vehicle, which was left standing on scene, was found to be registered to David Chow's father using the address of a Chinese restaurant in Manteno, Illinois—the same restaurant that had registered the getaway vehicle used in the gun collector's home invasion.

Evidence technicians working the Jade House restaurant robbery found that David Chow and his co-arrestees had tied up the employees with a rare type of marine rope. Investigators were able to track the rope to a purchase in Racine, Wisconsin. They further discovered that the same rope was used during another takeover-style robbery, this one at the Golden Dragon restaurant in Lyndhurst, Ohio. Dave Chow and three of his co-offenders matched the description in that incident.[169]

Detectives diligently working the Hip Sing gambling den robbery made six arrests of Ghost Shadow gang members. All six of the gang members were brought into the station to participate in a physical lineup. Hip Sing secretary Joseph Leung was present to view the possible suspects. Joseph Leung identified the men as the offenders in the Hip Sing robbery. However, Leung refused to sign complaints or to cooperate any further with state's attorney prosecutors. All six Ghost Shadow gang members were released without charges. It was clear to Chicago police detectives that, once again, this would be handled the "Chinese way."[170]

Chicago police intelligence found that the Ghost Shadows were having troubles of their own. During the summer of 1977, as law enforcement efforts heated up, the Ghost Shadows split in two. The split began as trouble brewed in New York City, causing an internal conflict of their own. The problems quickly spread to Chicago as many local Ghost Shadows refused to honor ranking members who came from New York City.

Most of the Chicago Ghost Shadows honored Andrew "Kojack" Lee as the Chicago leader of the Ghost Shadows.[171] He owned the Wing Sing Wet Wash near Forty-Third and Cottage Avenue on the city's south side. Lee had a bodyguard who also served as his driver, named Wai Kai Lou. Lou had come to Illinois recently by way of Racine, Wisconsin, but he was a known member of the Ghost Shadows from New York City. Lou drove his boss around in a silver Mark IV Lincoln that was registered to Lee himself. Recruitment into the Ghost Shadows had ramped up under Lee's leadership. The gang was constantly looking for new young members.

Law enforcement intelligence in Chicago had recently documented the arrival of members of the Wah Ching gang. Loosely translated to "China's Youth," the Wah Ching held a heavy presence in San Francisco but had never been documented in Chicago. The Wah Ching did not have the numbers to rival the Ghost Shadows, and it was later documented that most Wah Ching members changed their allegiance and became members of the Ghost Shadows. The Wah Chings had made a similar push for control in New York City. There, they aligned themselves with the Ghost Shadows in order to fight for territory in Chinatown, but intelligence suggested that, similarly to those in Chicago, the Wah Chings in New York City had either been eliminated or absorbed.

Around the time of Lee's rise to power, Raymond Ly left Chicago for Toronto. Intelligence suggested that he brought several Ghost Shadow members loyal to himself and attempted a recruitment drive.[172] Toronto authorities stepped up their pressure, and Ly settled back on the East Coast once again. Ly was arrested and indicted for various federal racketeering charges. His time in Chicago had been relatively brief, and other than being a suspect in the Hip Sing gambling den robbery, he had escaped any Illinois prosecution.

The new focus on Asian organized crime gave Chicago police authorities more intelligence, leading to more arrests. Baltimore, Maryland Ghost Shadow member Chin Si Chang was hiding out in Chicago's Chinatown, eluding federal authorities on a slew of more than twenty extortion- and racketeering-related charges. After a tip on a description of Chang's possible vehicle, Chicago police set up surveillance and arrested Chang as he attempted to enter his car.[173] Chang was processed and sent to Cook County jail, and the FBI was notified for extradition.

Andrew "Kojack" Lee later retired from the Ghost Shadows and took over as president of the nonprofit Chinese Consolidated Benevolent Association. During that time period, a private social group of Chinese Freemasons, headquartered at 211 West Cermak, quietly aligned with the Ghost Shadows. Lee cut off all ties to his former gang, essentially going "legit."[174]

CHAPTER 11

BEGINNING OF THE END

不善始者不善终

"A Bad Beginning Makes a Bad Ending"

Ghost Shadow leader Yin Pon "Nicky" Louie arrived in Chicago in the early eighties after fleeing New York City. Louie began his criminal career there as a street thug, battling rivals like the Flying Dragons and the White Eagles. Louie's big break came after being sponsored by Quat Kay Kee, a prominent member in New York City's Chinatown underworld who held a ranking position in the greater On Leong Tong. The On Leong learned the usefulness of Louie and his Ghost Shadows street gang, particularly in battling the White Eagles street gang, which had become something of a nuisance to the On Leong. After an incident in which a youthful member of the White Eagles showed disrespect to an On Leong elder by pouring water on him in a restaurant, the On Leong officially adopted the Ghost Shadows and successfully drove out the White Eagles from On Leong territory.

Street gang warfare raged in New York City's Chinatown, and Nicky Louie gained a tough reputation. He had survived several assassination attempts, and it was rumored he had been shot so many times that if you listened closely, you could hear the bullets clanging together when he moved.[175] But Nicky Louie was unsatisfied with his role as the leader of the street gang subservient to the greater On Leong.

Top: Author's rendering of Nicky Louie. *Harrison Fillmore.*

Bottom: Author's rendering of Eddie Chan. *Harrison Fillmore.*

Around the same time, Eddie "T.C." Chan—or "Fast Eddie" as he was coming to be known in some circles—had arrived in New York City. Chan was a disgraced former police officer from Hong Kong. Holding the rank of staff sergeant at the time, Chan fled the country in 1974 amid large-scale indictments for corruption. While on the run, he became known as the Sixth Dragon for his role in the police corruption. He settled in New York City, where he bought favor with the On Leong, buying several restaurants and businesses with what were suspected to be illicit funds he collected as a crooked cop. Chan's emergence in New York City's Chinatown and sudden rank within the On Leong did not sit well with some of the established members and certainly not with Nicky Louie, who demanded a sit-down.

The meeting began with Chan presenting Louie with ancient Triad hand signs. Louie scoffed at the gesture and told Chan something to the effect of, "You're in America now, that Triad stuff don't mean nothing here, you gotta pay."[176] Chan thought it best to pay the few thousand dollars to appease the street gang and came up with the money, which meant very little to the millionaire. But Chan was angered by Louie's disrespect and was aware of Louie's aspirations to take over the On Leong.

After the arrest of New York City's Benny Ong, recognized leader of the Hip Sing, Eddie T.C. Chan took over as Chinatown's underworld leader. Chan had been voted in as the On Leong's National President. Shortly after the election, Chan made it clear: Yin Pon "Nicky" Louie was out.

The Ghost Shadows split into two distinct sides. Many of Louie's trusted lieutenants sided with Chan. Violence erupted among the once-aligned members as the street gang's hierarchy deteriorated.

Louie survived yet another assassination attempt, this time by Ghost Shadow member Robert "Potato" Hso. The difference this time was that

The murder scene, On Leong Merchants Association balcony. *Photograph by author.*

Louie cooperated with law enforcement, identifying his assassin and aiding in the subsequent prosecution.[177] Nicky lost his credibility in New York City and fled to Chicago.

Ousted from his position in New York City and banned by the Ghost Shadows nationwide, Nicky came to Chicago to recruit for his own gang, the White Tigers, a gang with no affiliation to the Ghost Shadows or the On Leong. Louie did, however, make connections with the Chicago Hip Sing. He also recruited disgruntled ex–Ghost Shadow members and was open to working with Asians who were not Chinese. Louie attempted to make his mark in Chicago, starting an extortion scheme of his own using these new connections. He pressed his luck, venturing into On Leong territory. In a bold move, he ordered the beating of Chicago's On Leong's Fong Jong, or main enforcer, the powerful Henry Fong. Louie sent several of his henchmen, including Allen Li and Barry Chu—two enforcers he called the Action Boys—along with William Fatman Chin.[178] That incident would set up the "hit" and ultimate murder of Fatman, as described in the first chapter.

Eleven months after he'd been shot by assassins hidden on the balcony of the On Leong Merchants Association building, William Fatman Chin was pronounced dead, at 8:05 in the morning on the thirty-first of May 1981. The medical examiner reported that he died from injuries sustained from the shooting.

After an extensive investigation, detectives charged three members of the Ghost Shadows with aggravated battery. Lenny Chow, Paul Tang and Sik Chin had all been previously arrested and charged with aggravated battery. Now that Chin's wounds had proved fatal, Chow, Tang and Chin were indicted for murder.

Lenny Chow was represented by the infamous Chicago Outfit attorney Robert Cooley, who would later expose extensive corruption in the court system. Cooley was summoned to meet Chicago's unofficial mayor of Chinatown, Wilson Moy. The On Leong Association feared that a conviction might force its hit man, Lenny Chow, to cooperate with authorities, and he simply knew too much for that to happen. Wilson Moy reached out to then-alderman Fred Roti to fix the trial. Wilson Moy had been paying protection to the Chicago Outfit for years through Roti, but both sides were very careful not to show any association between Chinatown organized crime and the Outfit. Cooley was even warned, "Don't bring him around Counsellors [a restaurant Roti and his cohorts frequented] and don't meet him in your office, and when you meet him, don't indicate you have a relationship with us."[179]

Roti set the price at $100,000, $50,000 of which was to pay off the judge, and sent Cooley to negotiate. Wilson Moy paid Cooley $10,000 in cash up front, with most of it going directly to the Outfit. The On Leong in New York City sent an enforcer named Chan Kwok Wing to oversee the affair. Wing was a muscular martial arts expert, "barrel chested with legs as big as tree trunks."[180] Wing made sure that all the witnesses were available to Cooley before the trial. They cowered as Wing stood over them while Cooley coached them into changing their original statements to police. Cooley and Wing became regular pals out on the town in Chicago, while Roti and his right-hand man, Pat Marcy, dealt with the judge and his cut.

The trial became the proverbial dog and pony show, as the outcome had already been bought. All three witnesses changed their prior testimony under the threatening glare of Chan Kwok Wing in the gallery. After the assured not guilty verdict was read, Cooley was met by Wilson Moy, this time surrounded by others, in front of the On Leong Association building, mere feet from where Chin was murdered. Cooley was handed $40,000 but told that he had been summoned by the New York faction of the On Leong to collect the rest of the outstanding debt.

Author's rendering of Robert Cooley. *Harrison Fillmore.*

Cooley flew to New York, where he was met by what he described as Ghost Shadow "kids."[181] He later hooked up again with On Leong enforcer Chan Kwok Wing, who brought him to meet the formerly disgraced Hong Kong policeman and current National President of the On Leong, Eddie Chan. Cooley was paid the remainder of the bribe and enjoyed VIP status while he wined and dined in New York City. Thanks to his success in getting Lenny Chow off scot-free, the crooked attorney would later pick up several other On Leong cases around the nation. Local law enforcement had long suspected that the Chicago On Leong was part of a larger national network of Chinese organized crime, and Eddie Chan's involvement with the Chicago murder solidified these suspicions.

After the retaliatory murder of William Fatman Chin and after a semi-successful recruitment drive, Yon Pin Nicky Louie fled Chicago. Along with his new secret society, bent on retaliation and intending to retake Chinatown, he returned to New York City. He established his White Tigers in Queens and continued to take in Asian members who were not Chinese, including Vietnamese and Koreans. He attempted to work out a takeover peacefully, meeting with the current leader of the Ghost Shadows, Robert Hu. The meeting was unsuccessful, and it led to Louie's right-hand man attempting to assassinate Hu shortly after the meeting.[182] Taking over Chinatown was not going to be easy.

Before the White Tigers could seriously establish themselves in New York City's Chinatown underworld, a wave of indictments hit the Ghost Shadow members. With charges spanning a decade, Yon Pin Nicky Louie and his old Ghost Shadow gang members faced federal racketeering charges including extortion, robberies, kidnappings and a total of thirteen murders.[183]

The White Tigers did not last long in Chicago, and their allegiance to the incarcerated leader was most likely the reason they did not survive more than a few years as a criminal enterprise. The White Tigers never claimed any territory in the city of Chicago and were never officially connected to any crimes. The gang ultimately disappeared. Nicky himself never gained any real traction while in Chicago, but during his short time in the city, he managed to create chaos that would have dire implications in the years to come. Yon Pin Nicky Louie ordered the beating of Henry Fong, leading to the murder of William Fatman Chin, the event that ended up bringing down the entire On Leong criminal enterprise. Chicago police detectives may have been stunned by Lenny Chow's not guilty verdict, and while it may have felt like a victory to Wilson Moy, it would soon be the undoing of Chinese organized crime in Chicago.

CHAPTER 12

THE MOB MOVES IN

龙潭虎穴

"A Dragon's Pool and a Tiger's Den"

Back in Pittsburgh, Pennsylvania, Yu Lip Moy was a successful restaurateur. He was also the president of the On Leong, beginning in 1984. Shortly into his term, the On Leong's previous president, Gen Ping Moy, related that the Chicago Outfit had forced the closure of the On Leong's gambling interests in the city over a $12,000 protection debt and that it was now up to Yu Lip, as the current president, to solve this crisis.[184]

Angelo "the Hook" LaPietra met with Wilson Moy in the early 1970s. LaPietra had one very fine point to get across: if you want to gamble, you have to pay. Wilson Moy brought the chilling message to the On Leong board members, who decided, "Let's not fool with the mob."[185] Thus began Chinatown's rackets' protection payouts to the Chicago Outfit at $2,000 a month. Over the years, the payments were dutifully paid, on time and in full, but the price inflated until it was $9,000 a month. It was then that the On Leong found itself behind in the extortion payments.

Yu Lip Moy contacted a mob associate, Joe Sonken, who owned a mobbed-up restaurant called the Gold Coast in Miami, Florida. Sonken, in turn, organized a meeting with the Chicago Outfit's leading enforcer, Frankie Schweihs. Yu Lip Moy flew to Miami, where he met the infamous hit man on an oceanside park bench. He was then invited as a guest to Pittsburgh mafia boss John LaRocca's Miami home. A deal was hammered out arranging that the On Leong would pay Joseph "Jo-Jo" Pecora, a notorious Pittsburgh underboss, for setting up the protection meeting with Chicago, while Wayne Bock, another notorious Chicago Outfit hit man and partner of Frankie Schweihs, would collect $8,000 a month to pay toward the Chicago debt. Pecora would, in turn, send the money to Frankie and the Chicago Outfit for the privilege of operating underground gambling in Chicago's Chinatown. On Leong officer and manager of the casino Henry Fong approved the deal.

After Joseph Jo-Jo Pecora passed away in 1987, Yu Lip Moy seized the opportunity to change his payoffs to the floundering Pittsburgh mafia to $500 a week. However, the On Leong Association, mainly Henry Fong, continued to pay Yu Lip Moy $4,000 a week, assuming the deal was unchanged. Yu Lip Moy spent the next year lining his own pockets with the $3,500 meant to pay the Chicago Outfit. Admittedly, he gambled most of that skimmed cash away.

As National President of the On Leong, Yu Lip Moy traveled to oversee gambling operations in Detroit, Minneapolis and Atlanta and in Houston, which was the On Leong's fastest-growing market for Chinese gambling. He was allotted cash in what he would call "coffee money" for his visits. He was also paid $200 a week by Ken Moy, who, along with Henry Fong, was running Chicago's gambling. Often, he was supplied with gambling chips on the house or on credit. According to the federal government, the On Leong, at this point, was reaping close to $12 million in gambling profits around the country.[186]

Chinatown's gambling wasn't confined to the On Leong's casino. Joe Wing and his partner, Kenny Hom, were running a book and a number of wire rooms in Chicago's Chinatown. Serving only Chinese bettors, Wing accepted wagers on sports and horse racing. Wing's wire rooms were often set up in bare and vacant apartments. Wing recruited clerks to work phones for incoming bets and record the wagers on dissolvable slough sheets. Wing himself usually "settled up" with individual bettors. The most lucrative side of his business was his "juice loans," which extended credit to bettors with high percentages added on in "street tax." The street tax could keep a bettor underwater for long periods of time as the juice percentage grew.

If a bettor did not have the money, Wing would use strong-arm tactics, threatening harm if the debt was not paid. He and his enterprise were also backed by the Chicago Outfit. To quote Angelo "the Hook" LaPietra, "If you want to gamble, you have to pay."[187] The Chinatown wire rooms and bookies paid a percentage to the Twenty-Sixth Street crew of the Chicago Outfit, which fell under the leadership of Joseph "Shorty" LaMantia and his adopted son Aldo "Junior" Piscitelli. Piscitelli collected roughly 5 percent of all of Wing's operations.

CHAPTER 13

LAW ENFORCEMENT CATCHES A BREAK

正压百邪

"One Ounce of Justice Can Overcome Thousands of Evil"

Mob attorney Robert Cooley walked into the Chicago FBI offices on his own accord. While they suspected the attorney of being in bed with the Chicago Outfit, federal authorities had no open case on him, nor were they seeking charges of any kind. Cooley had been warned by close associates that he was no longer in favor with the Outfit and that there was a price put out for his assassination. Robert Cooley, fed up with the Outfit and the rampant corruption in the courthouses of Cook County, Illinois, decided to cooperate.[188]

Operation Gambatt began with Cooley wearing a wire for the FBI, recording meetings with Outfit leaders, politicians and judges. Cooley was clearly after the Outfit while exposing corruption in the justice system, but his efforts also—in a way, unintentionally—exposed Chinatown's organized crime.

Cooley had already collected evidence of the On Leong fixing the case against Lenny Chow and his Ghost Shadow codefendants, who murdered William Fatman Chin. In an unexpected turn of events, On Leong enforcer Chan Kwok Wing met Cooley in New York City. Cooley had come to know Wing during his work on the Lenny Chow trial and had gained a reputation for being connected to the Chicago Outfit. Wing brought Cooley to a ritzy high-rise in Manhattan. After Wing made a phone call from the lobby, the two were met by none other than Eddie T.C. Chan. Chan handed Cooley an envelope with a photo of an On Leong rival in Houston. Wing explained that the man had killed their "people" and that they were able to get his partner but not him. They were unable to get close to the target because he was suspicious of any Chinese hit men. They wanted Cooley to hire an Outfit hit man for the job because they believed their target would never suspect a white assassin. Cooley accepted the envelope and told the men he would see what he could do. Cooley later declined the contract.[189]

The next big break was the cooperation of Kenny Chu, the ex–New York City Ghost Shadow who, at the time of his cooperation, was the Fong Jong of Houston's On Leong. Kenny Chu collected evidence on both the Chicago and New York City factions as they fought for control over the Houston rackets. Chu cooperated after learning that there was a contract on the streets for his murder. There had already been three murders in Houston's Chinatown, and he feared a large-scale war. Chu was offered a murder contract by ex–National President Chan Wing Yeung. Yeung and his New York factions solicited Chu for the murders of Wing Tong Chin and Ah Tong. Chu cooperated with the FBI instead and later assisted with information to take down the national On Leong and its Houston, New York City and Chicago associations.[190]

The third big break for law enforcement, and possibly the most important, came when a man named Simon Au Leung came forward and agreed to become a federal informant. Simon was a man fed up. He was quoted in the *Chicago Tribune*: "I was convinced I had to do something for the Chinese people; over ninety eight percent are law-abiding but I could see it [drugs and gambling] getting out of control, getting bigger and bigger and stronger. I waited for someone to take care of the problem but it wasn't happening. I wanted to stand up."[191]

Wanting to "stand up" was a very brave motive, braver still in Chinatown's secretive underworld. Simon was already deep into the On Leong's gambling interests and was, in fact, employed as a dealer part time. When asked by the same reporter if he feared repercussions, Simon stated, "I'm not a minute afraid of them. I know their weaknesses. They are just like roaches and rats hiding behind innocent people."[192]

Armed with the new informants, the FBI began a full-fledged investigation into Chinatown's organized crime.

New York City law enforcement was building a case of their own against the On Leong in their own Chinatown. They flipped a small-time player into becoming an informant, and he testified to a grand jury that he knew

Author's rendering of Simon Au Leung. *Harrison Fillmore.*

the Lenny Chow case had been fixed. The underling did not have enough knowledge or evidence to corroborate his story, but it gave Cooley and his FBI handlers a jumping-off point to go after the case.

In the late spring of 1986, Cooley met with alderman Fred Roti's First Ward fixer, Pat Marcy. Cooley pretended to be afraid of the New York case and related to Marcy that he had the connections to retrieve copies of the grand jury transcripts. Pat Marcy was less frightened but took the bait. Cooley soon returned to Counsellor's Row, the First Ward's unofficial headquarters, this time wired up and with transcripts in hand. Cooley presented Marcy with the transcripts: "This little [expletive] punk is saying I told him the case was fixed. I never told anybody that we fixed the case."[193] Marcy kept a cool head but was captured on the wire confirming his involvement in fixing the case, even pointing out that he, Cooley, had gone to New York City to handle the payout. Cooley suggested they warn the judge in the case, because the judge had taken $50,000 to throw a murder case that was now in question in the federal theater. Pat Marcy dismissed the idea. "I ain't going to shake him up," he told Cooley.[194]

Meanwhile, Simon Au Leung was busy in the inner sanctum of the On Leong. As an informant, he was gathering intelligence and documenting criminal activity. When he wasn't working as a dealer for the On Leong, he was gambling within the walls of their gambling dens.

To enter the On Leong building, one would normally pass through the center doors on the east side of the building. But to enter the casino, gamblers were forced to pass through the heavily guarded doors on the southwest corner of the building. Armed Ghost Shadow gang members worked security at that entrance and communicated to other security members inside the building via walkie talkies. Once inside, cameras attached to a closed-circuit security system kept a careful eye on all who came and went. A second, locked metal gate entrance divided the first- and second-floor landings, and after patrons were buzzed through that, a third security door reinforced with concrete guarded the entrance to the casino. Gamblers allowed past that door were met by On Leong members to verify their membership. Only members or verified guests, vouched for by another On Leong member, were allowed.

A long Fan Tan table was closest to the entrance and often the most crowded. Just past that sat a large, twelve-person Pai Gow table with eight betting circles for gamblers to bet with or against the actual players. The mahjong tables were farther back in the corner of the casino. A recreational area with comfortable seats and sofas facing a number of televisions was located against the northern wall of the casino. It served as a place to rest or gain composure in between games. Adjacent to the rest area were tables for food and drink. Hot tea and coffee were always available, but liquor was seldom served. There was a soda fountain machine behind the serving tables, and light snacks were offered. On special occasions, more substantial food was provided, such as barbecue pork or roast duck.

In the center of the room, against the south wall, stood the cashier's window. The room was a cage with a teller's window and a large safe behind the workers. It was there that a gambler could exchange his cash for chips. Very few gamblers did so on credit, but it was allowed on occasion. It was well known and understood that if a gambler fell behind or owed money to the On Leong, there were serious repercussions.

The house took 5 percent of all winnings at the Pai Gow table, which generated approximately $3,000 in pure profit for the On Leong on a slow day. On weekends, special occasions or holidays, the cut could be as high as $40,000. The house take on the Fan Tan table was 10 percent, and that generated upward of $100,000 a day. It was not unusual for bets to be thousands of dollars at a time. The games were fast-paced, rarely lasting more than a couple of minutes. The gambling was frenzied at that pace, yet gamblers gravitated to the action and crowded those tables.

Profits on the mahjong tables were relatively low, sometimes less than $100 at four-hour intervals. This was due to the limited number of players at one table, coupled with the amount of time games tended to drag on. The On Leong considered those tables more of a leisure-type activity, putting up with them as a way to draw more gamblers in due to mahjong's popularity. The On Leong was betting that if a gambler came in to play mahjong, they wouldn't be able to resist the fast money and high-intensity gambling of the Fan Tan and Pai Gow tables.

Occasionally, other games were played, mainly at the four-person mahjong tables. A game called Thirteen Cards was one of the more popular games, but it wasn't unheard of for players to dabble in gin rummy or American-style poker games.

The room was filled with cigarette smoke, and the walls yellowed over time. The casino itself was very plain, with the bare minimum of decor.

It was crowded and loud; the chatter of the Chinese languages, mostly Cantonese and Taishan, filled the room. Many bets were placed verbally by gamblers over the heads of other players. On Leong officers walked among the crowd. Discrepancies were dealt with immediately but according to the very real mantra that the house always wins. The dealers were protected and often in debt themselves to the On Leong. The gamblers were almost exclusively Chinese.

The main ceremony room was located on the third floor of the On Leong Merchants Association building. The room had seating for over one hundred guests facing a large black altar. Taller thrones for ranking members stood closer to the front of the room. Atop the altar stood six urns, representing the Six Companies Triad from which the On Leong Tong was born. In the center of those was a grand statue of an ancient Chinese warlord. The urns were used to keep track of the On Leong's protection racket. Slips of paper with the names of local merchants and the amount of money to be extorted were kept in them. Some of the papers were pinned to a nearby wall. The room served as the central meeting place for the On Leong leaders and whomever else they had summoned.

The going rate for protection was $100 a month for a small business and $200 for something a bit larger. The payouts were sometimes referred to in code as "lucky money." Restaurants were charged $300 for the On Leong's protection. Often, the actual amount collected was $8 over the set price. This was Chinese superstition: the number eight rhymed with the word *prosperity*. New businesses also had to pay the On Leong for a "grand opening." The fee, which was between $1,000 and $2,000, was paid to the On Leong, which promised to bring customers for the event. Another soft extortion scam was the sale of good luck "moon cakes." Members of the Ghost Shadows would enter a business and offer a tray of special bakery goods for the low price of $108. Realistically, the goods cost the gang members under $10—if they hadn't stolen them outright in the first place. Besides the monthly poke, every restaurant was expected to serve Ghost Shadow gang members free food. Some of the more established restaurants ran $100 monthly tabs, allowing the Ghost Shadow members to order free food up to that amount. Other businesses would give more free food but only on a takeout basis. Extortion payouts were often made in a red envelope, for good luck.[195]

The long-term investigation into the Chicago On Leong brought to light many of the gang's secretive traditions and practices, many of which dated back to the days of Sam Moy and his brothers. It was estimated that there were over five thousand On Leong members across the country, with branches set up in fifteen different cities. Law enforcement officials discovered that the hierarchy structure of the On Leong was headed by two presidents, referred to as National President or Grand President. The presidents were elected at the On Leong's annual conventions. These conventions were held all over the nation, attended by delegates from On Leong groups from every represented city. Elections were held simultaneously for the positions of Treasurer, Chinese Secretary and, finally, English Secretary.

The English Secretary position was similar to the head of public relations. This position required a member who spoke fluent English, one who wasn't afraid to speak on camera or give public interviews. The English Secretary was also in charge of mutually beneficial relationships with politicians, judges and even the police. In addition, the English Secretary was in charge of translating books and records into English and of translating all business or government paperwork into Chinese for members to understand. The Chinese Secretary was the overall keeper of the On Leong's records, the great majority being in the Chinese language.

The Treasurer's duties were not unlike the tasks of a treasurer of any major business or corporation, overseeing the collection of membership dues and general bookkeeping. The Treasurer was also in charge of making sure the rackets paid their share. Any vice outside the direct control of the On Leong was heavily taxed, and any discrepancies in collections, debts or protection were handled accordingly. Those tasks were handled by the On Leong's Fong Jong.

The On Leong divided up into several groups of officers. The most active group was under the Fong Jong. This was essentially the enforcement arm of the On Leong. The officers of the Fong Jong acted on the orders of the presidents. They were in charge of maintaining order and control of all members. Recruitment was also the responsibility of the Fong Jong. Established members were always trying to find new members. Membership, they would pitch, meant you were a "shareholder," and the return on your investment was only capped at the amount of cash you wished to receive. Typical "shares" sold for $250 apiece. The rates of return were often sketchy, with the vast majority of On Leong members never gaining a profit. Successful business owners were strongly urged to buy more expensive shares, sometimes on top of their already costly monthly dues. The Fong Jong relied on a certain amount of strong-arm tactics and were responsible for overseeing the activities of the Ghost Shadow street gang and its members.

The next group was the Property Committee or Real Estate Group. It was responsible for financial investments, which were often in real estate, with the overall purpose of expanding the On Leong into other cities.

Houston, for example, became one of the On Leong's fastest-growing markets. The On Leong had been established in Houston back in 1934. In 1951, the gang built its own On Leong building, which had many architectural similarities to Chicago's but was never as impressive. The Chinese population in the 1980s flourished as upwards of thirty thousand new Chinese immigrants settled in the area. With the boom, gambling, prostitution and other vice rackets under the On Leong's control grew. A concerted effort on a national level by the On Leong began to pour resources and manpower into Houston, with the Chicago faction enjoying major control. Taking a page directly from their Chicago counterparts, Houston members turned their On Leong Merchants Association building into a full-fledged underground casino. Houston's faction paid $900 a week in gambling profits to the national On Leong.

The last group, and possibly the most important, was that of the Senior Elders. The Senior Elders group was composed of past presidents and other officers. They advised the current president and served at his direction. While a president might have the final say in important decisions, it was often at the behest or strong advice of the Senior Elders.

Treasurer and Fong Jong Henry Fong set up a shell company called the Koon Hing, which operated within the confines of the On Leong Merchants Association. The company's sole purpose was to launder gambling proceeds from the casino. On Leong officer Yick Norm Moy paid the Koon Hing a monthly "rent" to the company, ostensibly for use of the space in the On Leong building. The On Leong ran gambling dens off-site, as well. These were sponsored games in the backrooms of restaurants, laundries and social clubs. These On Leong–backed casinos were required to use official On Leong chips to assure gamblers of the credibility of the approved location. Whenever official On Leong chips were loaned out, they were expected to be returned at full price, plus the normal percentage of profits.

Trusted officers Chi Chak "Doctor" Leung and Ying Chun "Stephen" Moy were in charge of the daily tally of gambling winnings. At the end of every evening, one or the other would count the profits and hand over the tally sheets to Henry Fong. On a big night, both officers would report to Henry Fong. Before the money made its way into the casino safe, Henry Fong would skim between 5 and 10 percent to distribute later among the officers.

Author's rendering of an On Leong gambling chip. *Harrison Fillmore.*

Once a week, officer Yat Po Lau was given envelopes of cash out of the casino safe to pay each individual dealer. Approximately once a month, in the presence of Henry Fong and both his chief officers, money from the casino safe was transferred into the larger On Leong Merchants Association safe in the same building. With careful but secretive bookkeeping, gambling profits were first skimmed for the monthly payoff of the highest-ranking members. Then a portion was carved up to pay shareholders, biannually. Half the cash was left in the large safe for the On Leong itself. After ironing out those figures, Henry Fong tasked another trusted officer, Kenneth Dee Jin "D.J." Moy, with the hand-carrying of plain envelopes to the other leaders of the On Leong. The envelopes contained each ranking member's cut of all the monthly vice profits. These payouts frequently occurred in the Won Kow restaurant over dinner and drinks.

In the spring of 1985, Henry Fong made two withdrawals from the On Leong safe of $56,000 and $20,000, respectively. By October that same year, Henry Fong had withdrawn $130,000 to distribute to the officers and shareholders. The gambling business was growing rapidly, and by 1986, the twice-a-year payout for shareholders was over a quarter of a million dollars.

On March 14, 1986, the Chicago Police Department conducted a raid on the On Leong building. Acting on a tip and suspecting illegal Fan Tan gambling, they managed to enter the building and peer into the second-floor casino. The officers observed gambling, and they entered, announcing their office. A commotion ensued as dealers abandoned their tables, which caused players to grab what money they could, stuffing bills and chips into their pockets. Officers documented the raid and collected evidence of gambling: chips, wager slips and United States currency. Fourteen people were arrested, and the documented raid would later serve as a predicate act and evidence for a larger federal investigation.

The raid did nothing to slow down Wilson Moy, who served as the longtime English Secretary of the On Leong and who was still the recognized unofficial mayor of Chicago's Chinatown. In 1987, he was geared up for the biggest On Leong convention ever planned. The weeklong event was scheduled for the following year and was going

The Won Kow building. *Photograph by author.*

to be the year Chicago's On Leong pulled out all the stops to host the most-attended convention in recent memory. Moy traveled the country to ensure the attendance of On Leong members from other cities and factions. During an international On Leong meeting held in Taiwan, he boldly declared to On Leong leaders and officers that because of the protection afforded by both his own people and local law enforcement, gambling in Chicago's Chinatown was "one hundred percent safe."[196]

Convention plans expanded when it became clear that the Chicago On Leong building wasn't large enough to host the entirety of its guests. An even larger number of officers than expected was due to attend. Wilson Moy and the On Leongs decided to rent out a large portion of the Quality Inn

In the 1980s, the nation saw a large increase of "China White" in the heroin market. China White was known for its purity, far surpassing anything coming from south of the border. Opium cultivation and processing exploded in an area of southwest Asia known as the Golden Triangle. Deep in the jungles of the countries of Laos, Myanmar and Thailand were hidden square miles of crops of opium poppies. Much like the old traditions and legends that came with the Mafia and narcotics, many of the elder On Leong members steered away from profiting from the trafficking of narcotics. Many looked back on the days of opium dens with disdain and did not want it within their neighborhoods, especially around children. However, narcotics trafficking persisted, and while not exactly turning a blind eye, the On Leong expected to be paid tribute by any of their members who sold or dealt heroin or otherwise participated in the trade. Heroin from Southeast Asia was traded in units, rather than kilos. Units were seven hundred grams. One unit of heroin in the 1980s cost $80,000. If the buyer was not Chinese or had no affiliation to a tong, they could expect to pay over $100,000. The expanding business became so lucrative that some reasoned the success of the Asian criminal enterprises was comparable to the success enjoyed by the Mafia during Prohibition.*

* S. Sen, "Heroin Trafficking in the Golden Triangle," *Police Journal* 64, no. 3 (July–September 1991).

Hotel at Madison and Halsted on the city's near west side. Carrying out the plan was no small task, because the On Leong intended to run a full-blown casino with tables, cards, tiles and chips and planned to move large sums of money back and forth. It was Chan Wing Yeung's job to carry a briefcase full of cash back and forth between the Quality Inn casino and the On Leong building. He was authorized to exchange cash for playing chips and to front loans to trusted gamblers.

Henry Fong and his shell company assumed control of all the funds related to the 1988 convention. He hired new money counters, Chei Own Chin and Edmund Moy, whose only job was to count the poker chips given and received by the cashiers. Fong was also in charge of the manpower within the casinos. Expecting a larger-than-normal crowd, he hired officers Yick

Author's rendering of a map of the Golden Triangle. *Harrison Fillmore.*

North Moy and Shing Tom to work the room with him. He vetted every dealer, making certain they worked tables suited to their strengths. Fong knew a good Pai Gow dealer was not necessarily a good Fan Tan dealer. He was also in charge of the payments going directly to the Ghost Shadows for their security work, which were still being made on a weekly basis. There would be a need for extra security, longer hours and additional locations during the convention.

In the weeks and months prior to the convention, the On Leong attempted to tighten its books. The gang called on gamblers to pay any outstanding debts, as it would be critical to have loose capital the week of the convention. During that same time, amounts of credit were extended—some to as high as $10,000—by officers Dale Yee and Chi Cak Leung. The On Leong wanted to make sure gamblers also had enough to spread around. If there were any discrepancies, On Leong officers were consulted to settle the matter, ideally before the convention. The On Leong had a vested interest in settling all

Prostitution remained prevalent in Chinatown. While brothels and houses of ill repute had gone away, the industry had been largely taken over by "massage parlors." These tiny businesses were set up in storefronts all over the city and suburbs. There was nothing illegal about paying a woman for a nonsexual massage, and the businesses knew how to get around local prostitution laws. A customer would pay the house for a time-limited massage, maybe half an hour. Once inside the room with the masseuse, an arrangement for sexual acts was then made with the masseuse, not the house. This was a thinly veiled effort toward plausible deniability on the part of massage parlor owners. Law enforcement attempts were futile in tamping down what was largely seen by the public as a victimless crime. But there was a much darker side to these businesses.

Chinatown-controlled massage parlors were opened in the names of U.S. citizens, many of whom were merely fronts and had very little to do with the actual business. The parlors were often managed by an older woman who would arrange the initial transactions. The women who worked were often indentured servants. They had come into the country illegally searching for a better life, trafficked by Chinatown's criminal enterprises. Once in the United States, the women were forced to work off the debt of their own human smuggling. The debt owed was so high it lasted years to work off, in some cases. The rare arrest for prostitution resulted in the arrestee being trafficked to another city.

Human trafficking was a major problem in Chinatowns across the nation and wasn't limited to women. Men were commonly trafficked and then forced to work off their debts performing low-skilled manual labor in kitchens and laundries. The debts were similar in that it took years for the indentured servant to pay off the smuggler. Both men and women also had the option of smuggling narcotics into the United States as a way to pay their debt.

Many of the trafficking victims came from the Fujian province of China, which suffered from mass poverty. The going price was $30,000, an impossible fee for most. Victims were first brought to Bangkok, where they were given stolen Thai credentials or fake United States tourist visas. The victims were then sent to Bolivia,

Belize or Panama, which were considered good points of entry for eventual travel into the United States. The traffickers selected flights from those countries destined to Chicago, Miami or New York City, chosen for their crowded airports and overworked customs agents. Canada was sometimes used as an entry point, normally using someone else's credentials and assuming their identity to cross over. Illegal entry from Canada into the United States relied on the slower and sometimes lax border control. Crossing the Mexican border and using cartel coyotes was a last resort.

United States authorities broke up many human trafficking rings over the years. One incident was the meeting of a Chinese fishing trawler by a covert navy ship, which unloaded over one hundred victims at sea. In another bold attempt, human traffickers chartered a Boeing 707 and then painted it white to obliterate the markings. They purchased two hundred tickets from a European airline and attempted to fly into the United States pretending to be a legitimate flight.*

* "China Said to Clone 708 from Boeing Jet It Bought," *Washington Post*, May 9, 1980.

debts and solving any problems. If a gambler claimed the books were wrong, or if a gambler believed his line of credit was short, the matter was handled abruptly and diplomatically. Dale Lee and Chai Own Chin were called on to settle such matters.

Sheu Mon Moy was a regular gambler at the On Leong casino. When he caused a scene after an accusation of cheating, he was dealt with briskly and removed from the premises. Some time later, Sheu Mon Moy was snatched off the streets of Chinatown by members of the Ghost Shadows and taken to the On Leong Merchants Association building. Once inside, he was surrounded by On Leong officers and more members of the gang. The officers made it clear to him that they did not approve of his behavior and they intended to teach him a lesson. The Ghost Shadows severely battered the gambler. The police were never called, but Sheu Mon Moy would later testify in federal court as evidence of the On Leong's practices of extortion, intimidation and violence.

On Leong members and officers prepared for the weeklong festivities that surrounded the convention as well as the more serious business side of things. What Wilson Moy, Henry Fong and the rest of the On Leong coconspirators didn't realize was that Simon Au Leung, a high-ranking officer in the On Leong and a federal informant, was gathering evidence and feeding information back to the FBI during the preparations. And with this intelligence, the FBI was slowly building a federal RICO case against the On Leong criminal enterprise.

CHAPTER 14

THE RAIDS

罄竹难书

“So Many Crimes, Not Enough Bamboo to Record Them”

As current National President, Yu Lip Moy headed up several meetings during the conference where he sat down with all branches of the On Leong to report net earnings at their respective chapters. In the conference room, he and the ranking members held meetings with On Leong representatives from Atlanta, Detroit, Minneapolis, Pittsburgh, Boston, New Orleans and, of course, New York City. The officers handed in yearly financial reports, which included yearly earnings, holdings and future financial projections.

That particular year, the Houston On Leong was of particular interest to the national party. Houston's On Leong had long shared an interest with and received cooperation from Chicago's faction. Recently, Eddie Chan and his New York City faction were showing more interest in the growing market. The New York City faction had recently sent a Ghost Shadow fugitive, wanted for the shooting of a rival gang member, to hide in Houston while overseeing gambling operations. Houston's growing market allowed their On Leong members to simply expand their gambling interests and, in essence, open more casinos. This soon caused a conflict of interest as the underground casinos began to compete for the same gamblers. Houston's On Leong officer Chung Yiu Wu arrived in Chicago and presented Yu Lip Moy with the city's financial reports. Houston's On Leong was paying monthly tributes to both the Chicago and the New York City factions. There were heated discussions among officers regarding which casinos were to remain open, which should be closed down and who should retain overall control.[197]

Chan Wing Yeung arrived at the Best Western on time. Guests were enjoying the comforts of their hosts, and gambling was in full swing. At the nearby Maxwell Street Chicago police station, which housed the Gang Crimes Unit, a squad of gang specialists, detectives and patrolmen was gearing up for a raid. Acting on the reliability of a confidential informant and after logging hours and hours of surveillance, the team prepared to take down the gambling den.

On April 19, 1988, Chicago police officers raided the makeshift underground casino at the Best Western. Mass confusion would probably best describe the scene as gamblers and dealers alike scrambled for the exits.[198] Those in attendance were confused because they believed their safety was guaranteed by Wilson Moy himself. There was the underlying belief that the Chicago police had been paid off. Even Wilson Moy believed that his payments to the Chicago Outfit were, in part, to secure favor with the local police. Most likely, Moy's Outfit connections simply kept the payoff money for themselves. Someone, it seems, forgot to tell the Chicago Police Department. Several men were arrested on various gambling charges. In all, $30,000 in U.S. currency was seized along with a countless number of On Leong poker chips.

The Best Western raid did little to slow down the rest of the On Leong and its convention. The big games were still safe within the heavily guarded, fortified and surveillance-protected second floor of the On Leong Merchants Association building. The casino there kept running. It even became more crowded now that there was no secondary location for the conventioneers. The house was packed when the FBI conducted a raid of its own the very next night.

On April 20, 1988, confidential informant Simon Au Leung entered the casino. He brought with him two guests, for whom he had to vouch at the security doors. Both "guests" were sworn agents of the FBI. Simon had spent hours with the agents teaching them the rules of Fan Tan and Pai Gow, along with the courtesies and practices of how to make bets.[199] He laid out the floor plans for the breach teams, including details of the secured gates and entrances. He told them where the money would be, where the safe was located and who would be working the floor, more or less as pit bosses. Once Simon and the agents were inside and on the casino floor, they observed a frenzy of gambling activity. Bets were at a fifty-dollar minimum that evening. Some of the chips were stacked seven inches high on a single bet. Simon Au Leung and the agents split up, each working separate tables.[200]

The FBI teams arrived with an additional team from the Chicago Police Department's Internal Affairs Division (IAD). The department's IAD was assisting because it was rumored that local police were protecting the casino, and they expected to find on-duty personnel inside. The breach team made quick work of the entrance door and made it through the iron gate on the landing. There they were stalled, however, quickly realizing that the third door, the actual entrance to the casino, was reinforced with concrete. After striking the door unsuccessfully several times, it was clear that a sledgehammer or battering ram was not going to be enough to take down the door. One of the quick-thinking agents who had accompanied Simon into the casino simply walked to the door, opening it from the inside to allow the breach team entry.

Once inside, agents quickly dispersed among the crowd. Agents secured tables; two agents immediately secured and stood guard at the safe. Other agents located Henry Fong, Yick North Moy and Shing Tom, who had been identified as the On Leong officers working the room. Each man was found to be in possession of betting slips and thousands of dollars on his person. As the agents fanned out across the entire building, they discovered two secret tunnels, each leading to a different nearby building for a quick escape. A total of $350,000 in gambling money was seized that evening, with another $76,000 worth of chips.

The FBI found no Chicago police officers inside the building or in the casino. They did discover an off-duty officer who had been hired to work at the front door of the On Leong building, but they were never able to connect him to the gambling, payouts or any knowledge thereof. What they did find, in a briefcase near the safe under a bulletproof vest, was the confidential police report detailing the raid the night before at the Best Western.[201] It seemed there was no larger protection racket by police, but they did have a "mole."

Wilson Moy made a public statement that he had "no knowledge of a gambling operation" in the On Leong building.[202] Instead, he insisted, the FBI had merely interrupted folks inside the building playing four-hand rummy games. As there were no arrests made, Wilson said there was no substantial wagering. "It is a family game," he insisted.[203]

Gary Shapiro of the U.S. Attorney's Office begged to differ. He admitted that there were no arrests made, stating that the raid was conducted

Simon Au Leung wasn't only infiltrating the gambling and racketeering in Chinatown; he was working with federal agents to crack down on the narcotics trade, as well. Being trusted in the circles of the upper echelon of the On Leong afforded him credibility among those members involved in the drug trade. Using his connections, Yeung began to work an operation that would lead to the largest heroin seizure of its time.

Yeung coordinated a deal to purchase two kilograms of cocaine with a Chinatown elder named Joe Wing. Joe Wing once boasted of his control over the narcotics trade, bragging that he was the "only heroin dealer in Chinatown."* Joe Wing was connected to New York City's Chinatown through the notorious Peter Woo, aka Fok Leung Woo. Peter Woo approved the deals and acted as a broker between the dealers and sellers.

Simon Au Leung received a call from Joe Wing when the deal was set. Wing, speaking in code, related that Peter Woo told him the "shrimps" had arrived.† In a dingy west side motel room, Simon Au Leung met New York City dealer David Kwong. Under the surveillance of the FBI, Kwong sold Yeong two kilograms of cocaine for a total of $44,000. Kwong complained to Yeung that he personally was making only $3,000 per kilo, but he had been dealing drugs for a long time, and cocaine was moving faster than heroin.

With Simon Au Leung's connections, the FBI was able to introduce undercover agents posing as buyers. Using his trusted position once again, an undercover agent paid Joe Wing $35,000 for heroin delivered to a second agent in New York City. Once again, the deal involved Peter Woo and David Kwong. Agents were able to track the narcotics sales and determine their origin. During the investigation, Yeung traveled across the globe. Meetings were held in New York City, Toronto, Taiwan, the Philippines and Hong Kong.

In 1989, one of the biggest meetings in the global Asian narcotics trade was held back in Chicago at the Quality Inn hotel at Madison and Halsted. What the attendees didn't realize was that the entire

* "Police, FBI Score Nation's Biggest Heroin Bust," Associated Press, February 22, 1989.
† Ibid.

Author's rendering of Khun Sa, aka King of Opium. *Harrison Fillmore.*

meeting was being video recorded by the FBI. Simon Au Leung met with Chan Hok Peng, who was a lieutenant in the Burmese narcotics trafficking criminal enterprise under the leadership of Khun Sa, also known as "the King of Opium."* A deal was made for eight hundred pounds of pure heroin.

Months of investigation, surveillance and wiretaps went into what was dubbed Operation White Mare. The name of the operation was derived from the street slang for using heroin: "riding the white horse." The FBI seized a total of eight hundred pounds of heroin, hidden in car tires, from two separate locations in New York. The seizure was the largest to date, doubling New York City's "French Connection" bust years prior. A total of thirty-three people were charged in connection with the long-term investigation, including the seventy-one-year-old Joe Wing, Chicago Chinatown's top heroin dealer.

* Ibid.

only "for evidence of racketeering carried on through gambling and protection." Three months later, U.S. federal marshals seized the entire On Leong Merchants Association building.

With gambling effectively shut down in Chicago, the national On Leong turned its attention to the growing market in Houston. In the summer of 1988, Yu Lip Moy held several meetings to further the gang's casino plans in Houston. For a short period of time, the On Leong closed its casino on Dallas Street to open a larger, more lucrative casino nearby. Yu Lip Moy and Dale Yee met with other officers for the purpose of opening a new holding company with which to launder their casino profits. It seemed that the federal government had not stopped the On Leong criminal enterprise; it had just changed locations. But there was friction between the Chicago On Leong and New York City's On Leong over who would have ultimate control. Houston had been paying its dues to both factions, but after the raids in Chicago, New York City decided it would muscle in.

Several meetings were recorded by the FBI as the On Leong factions bickered over the business of Houston's gambling.[204]

Wilson Moy continued his role as a public figure and remained defiant. He spoke to the press and took on the damage control for the On Leong's public relations. As other ranking members scrambled for their bearings after the shock of the raids, Eddie T.C. Chan, suspecting impending indictments, fled the country. In July that same year, federal confidential informant Simon Au Leung, who had not yet been exposed, was summoned to the city of Manila in the Philippines for a sit-down with "Fast" Eddie T.C. Chan.

Simon Au Leung was invited to a fancy dinner at the home of Eddie T.C. Chan. At first, the dinner was cordial, with Chan proving a fine host. The evening turned sour after Chan accused Yeung of being an informant. Yeung professed his innocence, standing up to Chan's accusations. This angered Chan, who turned to threatening Yeung. "Horrible things happen to people who betray the On Leong," said Chan, according to Yeung.[205] Chan even brought up the William Chin murder as an example of those horrible things. Yeung pledged his loyalty, but it seemed Chan was unconvinced.

Chan, still hosting Yeung, brought him to a popular nightclub in Manila owned by another Hong Kong ex-cop. Yeung was brought to the backroom of the establishment, where he was introduced to the leader of a Taiwanese gang and his henchmen. After Chan slipped away, the leader offered to buy Yeung a drink. Yeung refused the offer. One of the henchmen drew a nine-millimeter pistol and pointed it at Yeung's head, calling him a traitor.[206] Yeung kept his cool, believing this was a test. Yeung was then able to disarm the henchman, which gave him credibility among the other gang members and their leader. Yeung was able to escape Manila unscathed.

CHAPTER 15

INDICTMENTS AND TRIAL

欲加之罪,何患无辞

"There's Always a Crime That Someone Can Be Accused Of"

In the late summer of 1990, the federal government announced the Chinatown indictments. At the top of the list was Chinatown's unofficial mayor, Wilson Moy. The National On Leong Merchants Association was also named in the indictment, along with its affiliated branches in Chicago, Houston and New York City. U.S. attorney Fred L. Foreman announced the thirty-four-count indictment of fifteen Chicago Chinatown defendants. The feds accused the On Leong of running an $11.5 million gambling ring using street gang members for muscle. The charges included bribing a Cook County judge to beat the Chin murder case, solicitation of murder, racketeering and tax evasion charges. Fourteen others were charged in the same complaint from various parts of the United States, including New York City's Eddie T.C. Chan.

Ranking members included current National President Yu Lip Moy; prior National Presidents Dale Yee and Chan Wing Yeung; Chan Kwok Wing, New York City's English Secretary; and Henry Fong, Chicago's Fong Jong.

Five indicted codefendants pled guilty before the start of the trial, including Sing Wing Jen, who, like the other four, was an officer in the On Leong but considered a minor player as far as the larger criminal enterprise was concerned. He pled to three counts of conspiring to run a gambling operation and tax fraud.

The Moy Association building. *Photograph by author.*

When the time came for the trial to begin, the defendants' lawyers let the public know exactly what they thought of the charges. The lawyer for Wilson Moy told the press, "These people are not criminals. They are not bad guys. It's a traditional thing to gamble. That's all it is."[207] Another attorney for the defense likened the On Leong to a McDonald's restaurant: "You can get a Big

Mac anywhere in the country."[208] The colorful trial was only just beginning as it became a Chicago-style criminal justice slugfest. After a particularly long and slow day, Judge Norberg asked the prosecution exactly how many witnesses they planned to call. The U.S. attorney answered, "Forty." The judge then asked, "Won't they be cumulative?" Defense attorney Rick Halprin interjected, "No your honor, they'll be Chinese."[209]

Wilson Moy was portrayed as a seventy-four-year-old man who occasionally gambled, as was common in his culture. With a deflection-minded defense, his lawyer insisted that Moy was actually the victim of the Chicago Outfit, which was running the gambling, and a victim of extortion by the Chicago Police Department. Henry Fong's lawyer portrayed his Fong Jong client as a small business owner and the victim of ruthless Ghost Shadow gang members who had nothing to do with the retaliatory murder of William Chin. Defense attorney Cynthia Giachetti compared the On Leong at large to a sort of "Moose Lodge" fraternal organization, stating, "This isn't a secret, sinister society."[210]

In accordance with his plea agreement, Yu Lip Moy testified on behalf of the prosecution. He detailed the On Leong's national organization and its gambling empire. Yu Lip Moy included information about the Outfit payouts and extortion and the fact that he had purchased bulletproof vests before the national convention for the protection of ranking members and those guarding the meeting rooms.

Lai Sang Mark was the assistant to the English Secretary from 1986 to 1988. Mark testified that in 1988, he was summoned to a late-night meeting in the On Leong Merchants Association building by Chicago president Edmund Moy. In that meeting, officers announced that police protection payouts had risen. National President Chan Wing Yeung learned from Henry Fong that the price had gone from $22,000 to $30,000. Mark himself was never part of any actual payouts, but he understood the money to be the price of business to keep the casino going and prevent police raids. Defense attorney Rick Halprin pointed out that On Leong members used the moniker "police" for anyone they paid off.[211]

The next to testify was Paul Tang, who had been acquitted of murdering William Fatman Chin along with codefendants Lenny Chow and Sik Chin. He admitted that they were members of the Ghost Shadows and acknowledged being summoned to retaliate for the beating of Henry Fong. Tang told the court that he knew the murder case had been fixed because Sik Chin told him that the On Leong spent a lot of money in doing so. Chin referred to the bribe, stating that it had been "cleared inside."[212]

The prosecution then called both Allen Li and Barry Chu, ex-members of the Ghost Shadows. At the time of William Fatman Chin's murder, they had all fallen under the leadership of Yon Pin Nicky Louie and his growing gang. Chu admitted to being a lookout with Li for the "Action Boys," as he called them, during the beating of Henry Fong.[213] Chu told the court that the beating was ordered by former Ghost Shadow leader Louie, who, he explained, had come to Chicago after losing a power struggle in New York City. Li stated that Louie gave no explanation for the beating.[214]

By the time Robert Cooley hit the stand, the case had been dragging on for over four months. Judge Norberg was clearly frustrated with the pace of the trial, and lawyers on both sides of the bench had become weary of each other. On the stand, Cooley told the court how alderman Roti bragged about his control of the Chinatown rackets, saying he "owned the Chinese."[215] Cooley went into detail about collecting money from On Leong officers to give to the alderman and his crony Pat Marcy to fix the murder case. During the cross, one of the defense attorneys became particularly combative after Cooley testified that before cooperating, he admitted his "bad acts" to the FBI. The attorney responded, "That took an awful lot of time."[216] Later during the cross, the attorney stood before Cooley and snarled, "I doubt you'd know an ethical lawyer if you saw one." "That makes two of us," Cooley snapped.[217]

The attorneys battled back and forth for much of the five-month-long trial. At one point, jurors sent a note to Judge Norberg, who had just about lost all his patience with the trial. The note pleaded with the lawyers on both sides to pick up the pace of the trial so that the jurors might "return to some semblance of normal life."[218] Judge Norberg was sympathetic and was quoted as saying: "I even feel sorry for myself."[219] The decision finally went to the jury, but after an excruciating ten days of deliberations, they were hopelessly deadlocked. Judge Norberg declared a mistrial.

Two years later, the feds reindicted ten of the original defendants. The complaint, which was described as "streamlined," contained only charges related directly to Chicago's Chinatown. It included Wilson Moy, Henry Fong and, in absentia, the fugitive Eddie T.C. Chan. All nine defendants pled guilty to lesser charges, several of which were tax related. More devastating was the seizure of the On Leong Merchants Association building. The loss of its headquarters, along with the grueling trials, eliminated the On Leong's dominance in Chinatown's underworld.

EPILOGUE

吃得苦中苦

"Enduring Deepening Pain Is How Man Succeeds"

In 1994, after the On Leong Merchants Association lost its building to the federal government, it reopened as the Pui Tak Center, partnered with the Chinese Christian Union Church. "Pui Tak" translates loosely to "cultivate virtue." The center hosts English classes and offers tutoring to neighborhood immigrants. Originally designed by architects Christian Michaelsen and Sigurd Rognstad, the building achieved landmark status and in the mid-2000s was awarded a $100,000 grant for historical renovation.

The center has a traditional Chinese school as well as an American-style preschool, the very first in Chinatown. There is also a medical clinic in the building, evidence that the building is being used again for its original purpose of aid and support for the community. On the second floor, where the smoky, clamorous casino once stood, a space is reserved to hold meetings for the center's Gambling Problem Program.

Without the building, the On Leong lost considerable power. Bookmaker Joe Wing, who had survived the first wave of charges in the On Leong RICO, was indicted for gambling and racketeering charges a few years later.[220] He was caught up in an investigation targeting the Chicago Outfit's Twenty-Sixth Street crew, which included Outfit boss Joseph Shorty LaMantia and Joe Piscitelli.

Crime in Chinatown had not disappeared completely. In the mid-2000s, another gambling ring was taken down by the federal government. During the operation, dubbed Tigershark, Dong Jin Chen and several others were charged with operating a casino above the Yeun Family Association at 211 West Alexander Street.[221] The feds also alleged they were running a juice loan racket. With no Ghost Shadows to rely on, the racket was enforced by a street gang called the Toi Chings. The Toi Chings was a subsection of the larger California Wah Chings, made up of Taishanese speakers in Chicago's Chinatown. Chen was sentenced to eighteen years.

In the winter of 2007, the U.S. Attorney's Office announced charges involving a large-scale narcotics trafficking conspiracy stretching from Toronto, Canada, to Chicago's Chinatown. One of the men implicated was Ivan Myint, an ex-member of the defunct Flip City street gang. He was working directly with two Chinatown middlemen, Thomas Man Lung Lo and Yong Ouyang.[222] Instead of opium or heroin, the defendants had been trafficking ecstasy pills and large amounts of marijuana, a reflection of the trends of local use.

Opposite: The Pui Tak Center as it stands today. *Photograph by author.*

Above: The current On Leong Merchants Association building at 218 West Twenty-Second Place. *Photograph by author.*

After the original RICO charges against the On Leong in the early nineties, the title "mayor of Chinatown" would never again be associated with being an underworld crime boss. Instead, the title, originally coined by members of the press, was bestowed on business leaders or successful restaurateurs. The new unofficial mayors of Chinatown did not oversee criminal enterprises; they were not "Godfathers" of organized crime. However, crime did seem to occasionally follow the title.

The president of the Chinese Consolidated Benevolent Association was a former deputy chief of staff of Mayor Richard M. Daley in the late nineties. Gene Lee was also president of the Chinatown Dragons Athletic Social Club and chairman of the Chinatown Summer Fair. Gene Lee was considered the unofficial mayor of Chinatown for much of the first decade of the millennium. He pled guilty to tax evasion charges and misappropriation of funds, having embezzled over $90,000 intended for the associations and charities. Facing up to ten years, Lee received probation.[223]

Tony Hu, the very successful businessman, was the head of the Chinese-American Association of Greater Chicago. He owned several high-end restaurants and was even lauded by then-mayor of Chicago Rahm Emmanuel, who was quoted, "Tony Hu has earned the nickname 'Mayor of Chinatown' for a reason" and called him a "valued leader in our city."[224] But in 2014, the FBI and IRS agents executed a search warrant on Hu's home, finding an "assembly line" of documented tax fraud.[225] Tony Hu pled guilty and was sentenced to forty-eight months in prison and ordered to pay over $1 million to the State of Illinois in restitution.

The New Chinatown Hip Sing building stands on Argyle Street today. Members liken it to a social club, where tea is served and friendly traditional Chinese games are played. The On Leong still owns a building in Chinatown on Twenty-Second Place. The nondescript brick three-flat is much smaller than its original "Chinatown City Hall." The On Leong remains a merchants' association with social services available to the community.

Human trafficking and prostitution remain a problem in the community. The Chicago Police Department's human trafficking team, aligned with the FBI, has had some success in breaking up smaller rings, nothing like the organized rackets of the past. Massage parlors seem to pop up regularly in random storefronts in Chicago and its surrounding suburbs. Very few of these establishments last more than a year in business after law enforcement targets them.

Bingo was legalized in Illinois in 1971. The Illinois State Lottery began in 1975. Both contributed to the end of organized crime's involvement in

Looking south on Wentworth Avenue from Cermak. *Photograph by author.*

lotteries and policy games. Riverboat gambling became legal in Illinois in 1990, and land-based casinos were legalized in 1999. While there are no casinos standing in Chinatown, buses chartered by local casinos line the streets, shuttling gamblers from Chinatown to their respective establishments. The Horseshoe in Hammond, Indiana, runs shuttles eight times a day. Michigan City's Four Winds' Golden Dragon bus line runs two shuttles a day, and the bus to the Rivers Casino in the suburb of Des Plaines runs three times a day.

A study by Professor George Knox, PhD, found that most Asian gang members do not belong to Asian gangs. Rather, they are drawn into larger, long-existing and more established street gangs. In the city of Chicago, they gravitate toward membership in the "People" factions of the Latin Kings and Vice Lords or the "Folks" factions of the Two-Six or Gangster Disciples.[226]

Street crews and youth gangs will always exist, as will crime in Chinatown. As of 2020, the Chicago Police Department's Organized Crime Bureau had no documented active "Asian" street gangs. And by all accounts, traditional Chinese tongs, and their associated "Godfathers" in Chicago, have completely disappeared.

NOTES

Chapter 1

1. Chicago Police Department, *Cook County Illinois Indictment 81-C-4020.*

Chapter 2

2. W.P. Morgan, "Triad Societies in Hong Kong," *British Journal of Criminology* 24, no. 1 (1984): 6.
3. Ulrich Theobald, "Chinese History—Han Dynasty," ChinaKnowledge.de, 2012.
4. Chi-Yun Chen, "Who Were the Yellow Turbans: A Revisionist History," *Istituto Italiano per l'Africa e l'Oriente* (1988): 57–68.
5. Elizabeth J. Perry, "Worshipers and Warriors: White Lotus Influence on the Nian Rebellion," *Modern China* 2, no. 1 (January 1976): 321.
6. P.M. Yap, "The Mental Illness of Hung Hsiu-Ch'üan, Leader of the Taiping Rebellion," *Journal of Asian Studies* 13, no. 3 (May 1954): 287.
7. Emily Wetzki, "We Talked to the Great-Grandson of Shanghai's Baddest Gangster," thatsmags.com, October 27, 2016.
8. "Boxer Rebellion," Encyclopedia Britannica, https://www.britannica.com, retrieved 2021.

9. "China Relief Expedition (Boxer Rebellion)," The Veterans Museum at Balboa Park, https://veteranmuseum.net, 2014.
10. Meir Shahar, "Ming-Period Evidence of Shaolin Martial Practice," *Harvard Journal of Asiatic Studies* 61, no. 2 (December 2001): 359.

Chapter 3

11. Dian H. Murray, *Origins of the Tiandihui* (London: Stratford University Press, 1994), 527.
12. Ibid., 522.
13. Ibid., 525.
14. Kam C. Wong, *Policing in Hong Kong: History and Reform* (London: CRC Press, 2015), 161.
15. Ibid.

Chapter 4

16. Raphael W. Marrow and Harriet I. Carter, *In Pursuit of Crime: The Police of Chicago: Chronicle of a Hundred Years, 1833–1933* (Sunbury, OH: Flats Publishing, 1996), 210.
17. Ibid., 211.
18. *Chicago Tribune*, August 14, 1874.
19. *Chicago Tribune*, September 11, 1876.
20. "Celestial's New Year," *Chicago Tribune*, January 27, 1884.
21. Marrow and Carter, *In Pursuit of Crime*, 212.
22. "Raid on Chinese Gambling Den," *Chicago Tribune*, December 26, 1894.
23. "Police as Ruffians," *Chicago Tribune*, February 20, 1894.
24. Ibid.
25. Ibid.
26. "Wah Lee Robbed and Jailed," *Chicago Tribune*, September 11, 1899.
27. Marrow and Carter, *In Pursuit of Crime*, 210.
28. Ibid.
29. David Burns, *The Life and Death of the Radical Historical Jesus* (Oxford: Oxford University Press, 2013).
30. "Messenger Boys Sent as Agents in Dope Traffic Is Charge," *Day Book*, October 14, 1914.

31. "Police Raid Opium Dens—Get Dope Information," *Day Book*, August 3, 1914.
32. "Revenue Agent in Chicago a Target for a Bullet," *Rock Island Argus*, November 13, 1919.
33. *Quad City Times*, August 23, 1900.
34. "News of the Day," *Day Book*, May 27, 1914.
35. *Chicago Inter Ocean*, August 23, 1915.
36. "U.S. Agents Trap 36 Tong Leaders on Dope Charges," *Chicago Tribune*, March 5, 1938.
37. "Wah Lee Mon in Court," *Chicago Inter Ocean*, January 13, 1899.
38. Karen Abbott, *Sin in the Second City* (New York: Random House, 2008), 142, 144, 147–48, 156.
39. "Women Smoking Opium," *Chicago Tribune*, March 13, 1882.
40. "American Women for Chinamen Traffic Shown by Police," *Day Book*, October 30, 1914.
41. "Chinatown's Lottery," *Rock Island Argus*, May 3, 1899.
42. *Chicago Tribune*, August 11, 1891.
43. "A Piece of the Heartland in the Orient," *Chicago Tribune*, October 8, 1989.
44. "Police Patrol Chinatown to Kill Killers," *Chicago Tribune*, October 22, 1924.
45. Marrow and Carter, *In Pursuit of Crime*, 211.
46. Edward M. Burke and Thomas J. O'Gorman, *End of Watch: Chicago Police Killed in the Line of Duty, 1853–2006* (Chicago: Chicago Books Press, 2007), 116.
47. Ibid.
48. "Washee Washee Gets Nabbed," *Chicago Tribune*, September 19, 1887.
49. Ibid.
50. Marrow and Carter, *In Pursuit of Crime*, 212.
51. "Terrified by an Oath," *Chicago Eagle*, December 2, 1893.
52. "Death to Be Chinaman's Fate," *Chicago Tribune*, March 17, 1893.
53. "With Rice, Gin and Firecrackers," *Chicago Tribune*, January 21, 1890.
54. "Flashback: Sam Moy, Chicago's First Mayor of Chinatown," *Chicago Tribune*, May 28, 2021.
55. Ibid.
56. Adam McKeown, *Chinese Migrant Networks and Cultural Change: Peru, Chicago and Hawaii, 1900–1936* (Chicago: University of Chicago Press, 2001), 145.

57. Ibid.
58. Richard Linthicum, *The Complete Story of the San Francisco Horror* (Chicago: H.D. Russell, 1906), 112.
59. Richard C. Lindberg, *Gangland Chicago: Criminality and Lawlessness in the Windy City* (Lanham, MD: Rowman and Littlefield, 2016), 68.
60. "Says Chinese Will Not Mine," *Chicago Tribune*, November 10, 1897.
61. "Sends Her Gems to Wash," *Chicago Tribune*, April 28, 1905.
62. Marrow and Carter, *In Pursuit of Crime*, 214.
63. "Sam Moy Sits in High Judgement," *Chicago Tribune*, February 2, 1894.
64. "Smuggling In Chinamen," *Chicago Tribune*, September 30, 1892.
65. "Lem Aut Is Ostracized," *Chicago Tribune*, August 16, 1891.
66. "War of the Washtubs," *Chicago Tribune*, August 19, 1897.

Chapter 5

67. Nathan Thompson, *Kings: The True Story of Chicago's Policy Kings and Numbers Racketeers: An Informal History* (Beverly Hills, CA: Bronzeville Press, 2003), 23.
68. Jesse Haney, *Speeches of Dennis Kearney, Labor Champion* (New York, 1878), 21.
69. "Chinese War on Clark St.," *Chicago Tribune*, January 11, 1895.
70. *Chicago Inter Ocean*, November 12, 1892.
71. "Allege a Conspiracy to Murder," *Chicago Tribune*, April 7, 1893.
72. "Wong Chin Foo Thinks Kern Opposed to His Family," *Chicago Tribune*, April 16, 1893.
73. Ibid.
74. Scott Seligman, *The First Chinese American: The Remarkable Life of Wong Chin Foo* (Hong Kong: Hong Kong University Press, 2013), 220.
75. McKeown, *Chinese Migrant Networks*, 199–203.
76. Lindberg, *Gangland Chicago*, 69.
77. "Flashback: Sam Moy."
78. Lindberg, *Gangland Chicago*, 69.

Chapter 6

79. *Chicago Inter Ocean*, May 26, 1908.
80. McKeown, *Chinese Migrant Networks*, 198.

81. "Our Chinese Pooh-Bah," *Chicago Tribune*, September 16, 1888.
82. "John China-Man Plays Baseball," *Chicago Tribune*, August 5, 1888.
83. Ibid.
84. "Homicide in Chicago 1870–1930," homicide.northwestern.edu, retrieved 2021.
85. "Chinese Murder a Maze of Plots," *Chicago Tribune*, June 7, 1908.
86. "Tells of Bargain to Kill Chinaman," *Chicago Tribune*, June 4, 1908.
87. Ibid.
88. "Chinese Murder a Maze of Plots."
89. Eric Trickey, "The Tong Wars," *Cleveland Magazine*, June 23, 2008.

Chapter 7

90. *Chicago Tribune*, December 1909.
91. "One Shot Dead in War of Tongs," *Chicago Inter Ocean*, April 22, 1912.
92. *Day Book*, June 10, 1912.
93. "Police Fear Tong War," *Day Book*, November 16, 1915.
94. "Homicide in Chicago 1870–1930."
95. "Chinese Murder Seen as Start to Tong Fight," *Chicago Tribune*, January 14, 1921.
96. "Police Patrol Chinatown to Kill Killers," *Chicago Tribune*, October 22, 1924.
97. Ibid.
98. "Chinese Gun Toters Spread Wide Terror," *Chicago Tribune*, October 21, 1924.
99. "Chinese Shot, Identifies Two Rival Tong Men as Assailants," *Chicago Tribune*, December 1924.
100. "Police Patrol Chinatown to Kill Killers," *Chicago Tribune*, October 22, 1924.
101. "Tong War Brings Second Slaying," *Chicago Tribune*, October 12, 1924.
102. Ibid.
103. "Chases Robbers," *Chicago Tribune*, February 6, 1927.
104. Ibid.
105. "Homicide in Chicago 1870–1930."
106. "Chinese Found Slain, Fifth in Two Months," *Chicago Tribune*, January 21, 1921.
107. Ibid.
108. "The Tong Wars."

109. Ibid.
110. "Fear New Tong War in Bombing of Laundry," *Chicago Tribune*, June 29, 1925.
111. "On Leong Chief Fires at and Nabs Six Men," *Chicago Tribune*, December 31, 1924.
112. "The Tong Wars."
113. Ibid.
114. Ibid.
115. "Homicide in Chicago 1870–1930."
116. "Gee Lum Acquitted," *Chicago Tribune*, December 18, 1925.
117. "Tong War Begins," *Chicago Tribune*, March 24, 1927.
118. "2 More Slain Here in Tong War," *Chicago Tribune*, March 27, 1927.
119. Ibid.
120. Ibid.
121. Lindberg, *Gangland Chicago*, 72.
122. Ibid.
123. "Homicide in Chicago 1870–1930."
124. Lindberg, *Gangland Chicago*, 72.
125. "Peace Pact in Tong War Made Public Today," *United Press*, August 13, 1929.
126. Marrow and Carter, *In Pursuit of Crime*, 214.
127. "Chinese Shot to Death as He Flees from Foe," *Chicago Tribune*, February 18, 1930.
128. "Chinatown Stirred as Café Man Disappears," *Chicago Tribune*, May 4, 1930.
129. "Blame Hip Sing Desertions in New Tong War," *Chicago Tribune*, June 8, 1930.
130. "Extra Police in Chinatown to Avert Ting War," *Chicago Tribune*, August 13, 1930.
131. "The Tong Wars."
132. "Assassin Kills Rich Chinese: Called Tyrant," *Chicago Tribune*, November 2, 1937.
133. "Chinatown Rites Pays Frank Moy a Final Tribute," *Chicago Tribune*, September 24, 1937.
134. Harry J. Anslinger, *The Murderers: The Shocking Story of the Narcotic Gangs* (New York: Farrar, Strauss and Cudahy, 1961), 47–52.
135. "Admits Bombing Welsher after Mah Jong Game," *Chicago Tribune*, January 13, 1939.

Chapter 8

136. "Heads Chinese Merchants," *Chicago Tribune*, March 1, 1942.
137. "Chinese Tong Secretary Sentenced to U.S. Cell," *Chicago Tribune*, July 23, 1931.
138. "Hunt Tong Clew in Slaying of Chinese Woman," *Chicago Tribune*, January 10, 1939.
139. "Mayor Moye of Chinatown Takes a Bride," *Chicago Tribune*, January 27, 1938.
140. Ibid.
141. "Slays Bandit," *Chicago Tribune*, July 4, 1946.
142. "Restaurant Man's Body Recovered from Lake," *Chicago Tribune*, October 16, 1950.
143. Calvin Chin and Gerald Moyes. *Ling Long Museum, Chicago Chinatown Visitors*. Promotional pamphlet published by the *San Min Morning Paper*, 1935.
144. "Local Chinese Loyal to U.S., Asserts Chief," *Chicago Tribune*, July 9, 1951.
145. "Deny Red China Demands Cash from Chicago," *Chicago Tribune*, July 9, 1951
146. Ibid
147. "Ask $80,000 Damages Over Mahjong Raids," *Chicago Tribune*, May 6, 1955.
148. "2d Chinatown Planned for Northside," *Chicago Tribune*, February 14, 1974.

Chapter 9

149. Ibid.
150. Chicago Police Department, *Asian Auto Theft Techniques*, November 6, 1989.
151. "A Ghostly Shadow Falls on Chinatown," *Chicago Tribune*, January 12, 1981.
152. "Tongs Strike Back in Chinatown," *Village Voice*, February 7, 1977.

Chapter 10

153. Chicago Police Department, *Y-067358*, February 28, 1977.
154. Ibid.
155. "That World We Call Chinatown," *Chicago Tribune*, February 5, 1978.

156. Ibid.
157. Chicago Police Department, *Ghost Shadow Gang*, March 24, 1977.
158. Chicago Police Department, *Y-049525*, February 14, 1977.
159. Ibid.
160. Ibid.
161. Chicago Police Department, *Y-293792*, August 11, 1977.
162. "Two Arrested in Extortion Plot," *Chicago Tribune*, August 12, 1977.
163. Chicago Police Department, *Ghost Shadow Gang*, March 24, 1977.
164. "Chinatown Ghost Gang Forays Spark Fears, Cries for Help," *Chicago Tribune*, March 1, 1977.
165. Chicago Police Department, *Ghost Shadow Gang*, June 28, 1977.
166. Chicago Police Department, *X-453738*, November 29, 1976.
167. Chicago Police Department, *Y-119267*, May 23, 1977.
168. Stratford Police Department, *77-042/004215*, March 13, 1977.
169. Chicago Police Department, *Ghost Shadow Gang*, February 7, 1977.
170. Y-067358, Chicago Police Department report, February 28, 1977.
171. Chicago Police Department, *Chinatown Alleged Gang Activity*, April 27, 1990.
172. Chicago Police Department, *Ghost Shadow Gang*, May 19, 1977.
173. Chicago Police Department, *CB #5185271*, March 13, 1978.
174. Chicago Police Department, *Chinatown Alleged Gang Activity*.

Chapter 11

175. Mark Jacobson, "Tongs Strike Back in Chinatown," *Village Voice*, February 7, 1977.
176.Jabari Gray, "The Ghost Shadows—Complete History | Chinatown Gangs," Forgotten Streets, March 8, 2021, YouTube video, 24:52.
177. "Nicky Louie Stops Smiling," *Palm Springs Desert Sun*, August 31, 1978.
178. *United States v. National On Leong Chinese Merchants Ass'n*, No. 90 CR 760, 1991 WL 30673, *17.
179. Robert Cooley, *When Corruption Was King* (New York: Carroll & Graff, 2004), 148.
180. Ibid., 150.
181. Ibid., 156.
182. Gray, "The Ghost Shadows."
183. *United States v. Louie*, 625 F. Supp. 1327-SDNY-1985.

Chapter 12

184. *United States v. National On Leong Chinese Merchants Ass'n.*
185. "Chinatown Defense Centers on Extortion," *Chicago Sun-Times*, April 9, 1991.
186. *United States v. National On Leong Chinese Merchants Ass'n.*
187. *United States v. Joe Wing*, 97-1731.

Chapter 13

188. Cooley, *When Corruption Was King*, 3.
189. Ibid., 167.
190. U.S. Congress, *Asian Organized Crime*, 47.
191. "FBI Witness Details Double Life," *Chicago Tribune*, February 11, 1991.
192. Ibid.
193. Cooley, *When Corruption Was King*, 200.
194. Ibid.
195. U.S. Congress, *Asian Organized Crime*, 47.
196. "Feds Hit Chinatown," *Chicago Sun-Times*, August 31, 1990.

Chapter 14

197. *United States v. National On Leong Chinese Merchants Ass'n.*
198. Ibid.
199. "Chinatown Gambling Inside Story," *Chicago Sun-Times*, September 2, 1990.
200. "FBI Informant Now Lives Unprotected—But Carefully," *Chicago Tribune*, September 2, 1990.
201. "Alleged Chinatown Gambling Included Bullet Proof Vests," *Chicago Defender*, April 11, 1991; "Police Report Found in Chinatown Raid," *Chicago Tribune*, March 24, 1988.
202. "Chinatown Gambling Raid Nets $350,000," *Chicago Tribune*, April 22, 1988.
203. Ibid.
204. *United States v. National On Leong Chinese Merchants Ass'n.*
205. "Chinatown Gambling Inside Story," *Chicago Sun-Times*, September 2, 1990.
206. "FBI Informant Now Lives Unprotected."

Chapter 15

207. "Chinatown Gambling Goes to the Jury," *Chicago Sun-Times*, August 13, 1991.
208. Ibid.
209. "Chasing a New Type of Mob," *LA Times*, May 20, 1991.
210. "Witness Tells of On Leong Gambling," *Chicago Sun-Times*, April 10, 1991.
211. "On Leong Witness Tells of Police Payoffs," *Chicago Sun-Times*, April 19, 1991.
212. "Witness to Slaying Describes Chinatown Merchants' Bribery," *Chicago Tribune*, June 20, 1991.
213. Ibid.
214. Ibid.
215. "Cooley, Lawyer Trade Insults in On Leong Cross-Examination," *Chicago Tribune*, July 3, 1991.
216. Ibid.
217. Cooley, *When Corruption Was King*, 278.
218. "On Leong Trial Too Long for Judge," *Chicago Tribune*, August 29, 1991.
219. Ibid.

Epilogue

220. *United States v. LaMantia*, 94-2667.
221. "Feds Claim Gambling Ring Broken Up," *Northwest Indiana Times*, August 22, 2003.
222. "21 Charged in International Ecstasy Bust," *Chicago Tribune*, December 7, 2007.
223. U.S. Department of Justice, "Chinatown Leader Pleads Guilty to Theft from Charity and Filing False Federal Income Tax Return," press release, April 8, 2014.
224. "Chef Had Assembly Line of Cooking Sales Record," *Chicago Tribune*, November 2, 2016.
225. Ibid.
226. George Knox, *An Introduction to Gangs* (Chicago: New Chicago School Press, 2006).

———. *Y-049525*. February 14, 1977.
———. *Y-067358*. February 28, 1977.
———. *Y-119267*. May 23, 1977.
———. *Y-293792*. August 11, 1977.
Chicago Sun-Times.
Chicago Tribune.
Chin, Calvin, and Gerald Moyes. *Ling Long Museum, Chicago Chinatown Visitors*. Promotional pamphlet published by the *San Min Morning Paper*, 1935.
Cooley, Robert. *When Corruption Was King*. New York: Carroll & Graff, 2004.
Courtwright, David T. *Dark Paradise*. Cambridge, MA: Harvard University Press, 2001.
Day Book.
Encyclopedia Britannica. "Boxer Rebellion." https://www.britannica.com.
Eng, Monica. "What's the History of Chinese Gangs in Chicago?" *Curious City* podcast, WBEZ, May 5, 2018.
Gray, Jabari. "The Ghost Shadows—Complete History | Chinatown Gangs." Forgotten Streets, March 8, 2021, YouTube video, 24:52.
Haney, Jesse. *Speeches of Dennis Kearney, Labor Champion*. New York: 1878.
Harland, Robert O. *The Vice Bondage of a Great City or The Most Wicked City in the World*. Chicago: Young People's Civic League, 1913.
Jacobson, Mark. "Tongs Strike Back in Chinatown." *Village Voice*, February 7, 1977.
Knox, George. *An Introduction to Gangs*. Chicago: New Chicago School Press, 2006.
LA Times.
Lindberg, Richard. *Gangland Chicago: Criminality and Lawlessness in the Windy City.* Lanham, MD: Rowman and Littlefield, 2016.
Linthicum, Richard. *The Complete Story of the San Francisco Horror*. Chicago: H.D. Russell, 1906.
Marrow, Raphael W., and Harriet I. Carter. *In Pursuit of Crime: The Police of Chicago: Chronicle of a Hundred Years, 1833–1933*. Sunbury, OH: Flats Publishing, 1996.
McKeown, Adam. *Chinese Migrant Networks and Cultural Change: Peru, Chicago, and Hawaii, 1900–1936*. Chicago: University of Chicago Press, 2001.
Morgan, W.P. "Triad Societies in Hong Kong." *British Journal of Criminology* 24, no. 1 (1984).
Murray, Dian H. *The Origins of the Tiandihui*. London: Stratford University Press, 1994.
New York Times.
Northwest Indiana Times.
Palm Springs Desert Sun.

BIBLIOGRAPHY

Abbott, Karen. *Sin in the Second City*. New York: Random House, 2008.

Anslinger, Harry J. *The Murderers: The Shocking Story of the Narcotic Gangs*. New York: Farrar, Strauss and Cudahy, 1961.

Associated Press.

Burke, Edward M., and Thomas J. O'Gorman. *End of Watch: Chicago Police Killed in the Line of Duty, 1853–2006*. Chicago: Chicago Books Press, 2007.

Burns, David. *The Life and Death of the Radical Historical Jesus*. Oxford: Oxford University Press, 2013.

Chee-Beng, Tan. *Routledge Handbook of the Chinese Diaspora*. New York: Routledge Taylor & Francis Group, 2013.

Chen, Chi-Yun. "Who Were the Yellow Turbans: A Revisionist History." *Istituto Italiano per l'Africa e l'Oriente* (1988): 57–68.

Chicago Daily News.

Chicago Daily Tribune.

Chicago Defender.

Chicago Eagle.

Chicago Inter Ocean.

Chicago Police Department. *Asian Auto Theft Techniques*. November 6, 1989.

———. *CB #5185271*. March 13, 1978

———. *Chinatown Alleged Gang Activity*. April 27, 1990.

———. *Cook County Illinois Indictment 81-C-4020.*

———. *Ghost Shadow Gang*. February 7, 1977.

———. *Ghost Shadow Gang*. March 24, 1977.

———. *Ghost Shadow Gang*, May 19, 1977.

———. *Ghost Shadow Gang*. June 28, 1977.

———. *X-453738*. November 29, 1976.

Perry, Elizabeth J. "Worshipers and Warriors: White Lotus Influence on the Nian Rebellion." *Modern China* 2, no. 1 (January 1976).

Quad City Times.

Rock Island Argus.

Seligman, Scott. *The First Chinese American: The Remarkable Life of Wong Chin Foo*. Hong Kong: Hong Kong University Press, 2013.

Sen, S. "Heroin Trafficking in the Golden Triangle." *Police Journal* 64, no. 3 (July–September 1991): 241–87.

Shahar, Meir. "Ming-Period Evidence of Shaolin Martial Practice." *Harvard Journal of Asiatic Studies* 61, no. 2 (December 2001): 359–413.

Stratford Police Department. *77-042/004215*. March 13, 1977.

Theobald, Ulrich. "Chinese History—Han Dynasty." ChinaKnowledge.de, 2012.

Thompson, Nathan. *Kings: The True Story of Chicago's Policy Kings and Numbers Racketeers: An Informal History*. Beverly Hills, CA: Bronzeville Press, 2003.

Trickey, Eric. "The Tong Wars." *Cleveland Magazine*, June 23, 2008.

United Press.

U.S. Congress. *Asian Organized Crime: Hearing before the Senate Permanent Subcommittee on Investigations of the Committee on Governmental Affairs, 102nd Congress, 1st Session, October 3, November 5–6, 1991*. Washington, D.C.: U.S. Government Printing Office, 1992.

United States Department of Justice. "Chinatown Leader Pleads Guilty to Theft from Charity and Filing False Federal Income Tax Return." Press release, April 8, 2014.

United States v. Joe Wing, 97-1731.

United States v. LaMantia, 94-2667.

United States v. Louie, 625 F. Supp. 1327-SDNY-1985.

United States v. National On Leong Chinese Merchants Ass'n, No. 90 CR 760, 1991 WL 30673, *17.

The Veterans Museum at Balboa Park. "China Relief Expedition (Boxer Rebellion)." https://veteranmuseum.net.

Village Voice.

Washington Post.

Wetzki, Emily. "We Talked to the Great-Grandson of Shanghai's Baddest Gangster." thatsmags.com, October 27, 2016.

Wong, Kam C. *Policing in Hong Kong: History and Reform*. London: CRC Press, 2015.

Yap, P.M. "The Mental Illness of Hung Hsiu-Ch'üan, Leader of the Taiping Rebellion." *Journal of Asian Studies* 13, no. 3 (May 1954): 287–304.

ABOUT THE AUTHOR

Harrison Fillmore is the nom de plume of a highly decorated and well-experienced member of the city of Chicago's law enforcement community. Having spent nearly twenty-five years investigating organized crime and considered an expert in the courts, Harrison Fillmore has been researching and collecting historical documents throughout his career, including those containing much of the information filling the narrative of this book.